THE CAMBRIDGE BIBLE COMMENTARY
NEW ENGLISH BIBLE

GENERAL EDITORS
P. R. ACKROYD, A. R. C. LEANEY, J. W. PACKER

A LETTER TO HEBREWS

THE CAMBRIDGE BIBLE COMMENTARY

A LETTER TO
HEBREWS

COMMENTARY BY

J.H.DAVIES

Lecturer in Theology
University of Southampton

CAMBRIDGE
AT THE UNIVERSITY PRESS
1967

Published by the Syndics of the Cambridge University Press
Bentley House, 200 Euston Road, London, N.W. 1
American Branch: 32 East 57th Street, New York, N.Y. 10022

© Cambridge University Press 1967

Library of Congress Catalogue Card Number: 67–18311

Printed in Great Britain
at the University Printing House, Cambridge
(Brooke Crutchley, University Printer)

GENERAL EDITORS' PREFACE

The aim of this series is to provide the text of the New English Bible closely linked to a commentary in which the results of modern scholarship are made available to the general reader. Teachers and young people preparing for such examinations as the General Certificate of Education at Ordinary or Advanced Level in Britain, and similar qualifications elsewhere, have been especially kept in mind. The commentators have been asked to assume no specialized theological knowledge, and no knowledge of Greek and Hebrew. Bare references to other literature and multiple references to other parts of the Bible have been avoided. Actual quotations have been given as often as possible.

Within these quite severe limits each commentator attempts to set out the main findings of recent New Testament scholarship, and to describe the historical background to the text. The main theological content of the New Testament is also critically discussed.

Much attention has been given to the form of the volumes. The aim is to produce books each of which will be read consecutively from first to last page. The introductory material leads naturally into the text, which itself leads into the alternating sections of commentary.

The series is prefaced by a volume—*Understanding the New Testament*—which outlines the larger historical background, says something about the growth and transmission of the text, and answers the question 'Why should we study the New Testament?' Another volume—*The New Testament Illustrated*—contains maps, diagrams and photographs.   P.R.A.   A.R.C.L.   J.W.P.

COMMENTATOR'S PREFACE

I should like to express my gratitude for the opportunity of writing a commentary on Hebrews, and my thanks to all whose work has enabled me to do so—the General Editors, whose experienced judgement greatly helped the writing of the commentary: my wife, who typed it: the Cambridge University Press, who with patient skill turned it into a book: the many previous commentators from whom I have profited: and the unknown writer whose work I have ventured to comment upon, becoming, as I did so, ever more conscious of its greatness.

Readers of this commentary will find that they are asked to do a good deal of close and detailed study. But there is no other road to a real understanding of Hebrews: and the journey is full of the pleasure of new discoveries.

J. H. D.

CONTENTS

A LETTER TO
HEBREWS

✳ ✳ ✳ ✳ ✳ ✳ ✳ ✳ ✳ ✳ ✳ ✳ ✳

SOMETHING RICH AND STRANGE

At first reading, the Letter to Hebrews will probably both attract and perplex us. It is like a work of art from another time and place—a mediaeval stained-glass window, for example, whose general meaning and beauty are clear enough, but whose style and details are strange and puzzling. We can better understand and appreciate such a window if we learn something about Christian art in the Middle Ages, and if we look longer and harder at the window itself.

Hebrews is a work of art. It may well attract us with its magnificent language, its vivid images, and the sweep and subtlety of its argument: but its world of ideas and its methods of reasoning are so different from those of today that we shall probably feel that we are missing a great deal of its meaning. The remedy is the same as for the mediaeval window. We must learn about its background—its purpose, its world of ideas, its methods of construction—and we must look attentively at the thing itself.

In the first pages of this commentary, then, we shall consider the background of Hebrews, for which we can draw upon the knowledge of many scholars about the history and thought of the ancient world, including that of early Christianity. Then we shall turn to the text of the letter, and study it in some detail.

THE TITLE OF THE LETTER

The title appears, with minor variations, in all the early manuscripts. The earliest reference to it is by Clement of Alexandria in about A.D. 180, so that the title may be much later than the letter. Three unusual things suggest that it was: (*a*) it does not name the writer; (*b*) it gives the readers no name, but only the description 'Hebrews'; (*c*) this description does not occur in the letter itself.

The title therefore seems to be a later attempt to explain the purpose of the letter, after this had become unknown. It was probably no more than a deduction from the contents of the letter.

WAS IT ORIGINALLY A LETTER?

The New Testament letters, following the custom of their time, usually begin with the names of the writer and readers and end with personal messages for individuals. Hebrews, however, plunges straight into its subject, and at the end gives greetings only of a general kind, apart from a message about 'our brother Timothy' and greetings 'from our Italian friends'. This has led to the suggestion that it was originally a sermon or tract, and was subsequently adapted to serve as a letter. But the writer has a particular group of readers in mind, since he refers to their past experiences, warns them of a particular danger, and seems to have designed the whole letter to fit their special needs. So we conclude that it was a letter from the first, and that there were reasons for the lack of names. The writer may not have known his readers closely or individually, or may have preferred not to name individuals. They would probably know his name, because it would be given by the person who delivered the letter.

THE MEANING OF THE NAME 'HEBREWS'

'Hebrews' could mean people who spoke Hebrew, as in Acts 6: 1, where the N.E.B. translates it 'those who spoke the language of the Jews'. But if the title is a deduction from the contents of the letter, the word 'Hebrews' is likely to have the more usual sense of members of the Jewish nation, who believed themselves to be specially chosen by God. Paul means this when he asks, in 2 Cor. 11: 22, 'Are they Hebrews? So am I. Israelites? So am I. Abraham's descendants? So am I.'

But it is clear from the letter itself that it is written to Christians: so the title probably means 'Jewish Christians', as distinct from gentile (i.e. non-Jewish) Christians. The author of the title may have thought that the letter was written about the special problems of Jewish converts to Christianity.

WHY WAS THE LETTER WRITTEN?

At this point we leave the title, and ask if the letter itself indicates who its readers were. It gives no direct answer, and we must therefore look for an indirect one. The best starting-point is to ask what purpose the letter was written for. Two points emerge as we read it through:

(*a*) The writer calls his letter an 'exhortation' (13: 22): the Greek word could also be translated 'encouragement' or 'appeal'. All three translations correspond to something in the letter, which contains passages of grave warning and of bracing encouragement, and which has the practical purpose of strengthening the readers' Christian loyalty.

(*b*) We find that the entire letter is an argument that Christianity supersedes Judaism. Evidently the readers have not fully grasped this truth, or are losing their grasp of it, and the writer is seeking to remedy this.

These two points are so interwoven that the natural conclusion is that they are two aspects of one and the same purpose. The writer is trying to strengthen his readers' faith by convincing

3

them that Christianity renders Judaism obsolete. The readers are facing some sort of crisis connected with these two religions. We now ask what exactly the crisis was, though in so doing we move on to less certain ground.

WHAT CRISIS WERE THE READERS FACING?

It will help us if we first consider what we know of the early history of Christianity from sources other than Hebrews.

1. *The General Situation in the Early Church*

Two relevant situations are known to us:

(*a*) Christians were suspected by other religious bodies—particularly the Jews—and by the Roman authorities. The local representatives of any of these might be hostile, and Christians anywhere might weaken and fall away under such pressure. A letter stressing the finality and all-sufficiency of Christianity would strengthen them.

(*b*) The chief difficulty in the first decades was the relationship between Jews and Christians. All Christians, whether Jew or Gentile by race, believed that God had made the Old Covenant with Israel, and that out of it he had made a New Covenant in Jesus Christ. Had they any obligations to Judaism now? Must they be Jews as well as Christians? How should they regard the non-Christian Jews, whose leaders had brought about Jesus' death? Such perplexities might weaken any group of Christians, and a letter suggesting the finality and all-sufficiency of Christianity, in explicit contrast to Judaism, would strengthen them.

2. *Particular Crises*

There are two particular crises that might well lie behind Hebrews:

(*a*) The readers may be dismayed at the idea that Christianity means the abandonment of Judaism. Those who valued the Old Covenant most positively would need to be assured that the New Covenant contained all that the Old did, and, even more, was its true fulfilment. Such assurance our letter seeks to provide.

A specially acute occasion for such dismay, often mentioned in connection with Hebrews, is the Fall of Jerusalem in A.D. 70. This destruction of the Holy City and Temple, and the ending of the sacrifices offered there, must have been a terrible shock to any Jew, even a Christian Jew. To such people our letter would come as a reassurance, telling them that the true sacrifice had been offered by Jesus, and that he was the true High Priest in the true, the heavenly, sanctuary.

The serious objection to this is that Hebrews nowhere mentions the Fall of Jerusalem, nor even the Temple itself. The sanctuary of the Jews is, throughout the letter, taken to be the sacred tent of the period of the desert wanderings under Moses. It is hard to believe that even such a subtle writer as ours could say nothing of the Fall of Jerusalem if it were the true reason for the letter. The only explanation would be that it was so fresh in his and his readers' minds that there was no need to mention it: but this seems most unlikely.

(*b*) The readers may be considering turning from Christianity to Judaism. This would explain why the letter argues that Christianity supersedes Judaism in particular: it is hard to see why it should do so unless the readers were weakening towards Judaism specifically. This would perhaps be the best explanation of the extraordinary harshness of the writer's warnings about the consequences of infidelity: if his readers were thinking of joining the very community which, in the Christian view, had rejected the Son of God, he might well describe such a desertion as 'crucifying again the Son of God' (Hebrews 6: 6, following the N.E.B. footnote).

This latter view seems the best one to the present commentator.

WERE THE READERS JEWISH OR GENTILE CHRISTIANS?

The view just adopted does not mean that the readers must have been Jews before their conversion to Christianity. Any of the situations described above could apply equally well to Christians who were Jews by race and to those who were Gentiles but had a strong sense of their spiritual ancestry in Israel. There are in fact two indications that the readers were Gentiles:

(*a*) The writer never says or implies that their turning away would be a turning *back*, as he surely would if they had been Jews before conversion. Judaism is presented as an obsolete religion, but not as their own previous religion.

(*b*) The warning about holiness of life in 12: 14, and about sexual immorality in 13: 4, seems unlikely to be directed to Jews, who were conspicuous in the ancient world for their ethical religion and their standards of sexual morality. Doubtless some Jews fell short of their standards, but these passages would fit the situation of Gentiles rather better.

We conclude that the readers were a group of gentile Christians under pressure to embrace Judaism. We read of such pressure being applied to gentile Christians in Acts 15: 1 and Galatians 3: 1 — 5: 1. If this conclusion is correct, the title 'To Hebrews' was a mistake, though an understandable one.

WHO WERE THE READERS?

We ask now what particular church this group of gentile Christians may have belonged to. We mention three of the many theories that have been advanced.

(*a*) *The Church at Rome.* In about A.D. 95 an elder or bishop of the church in Rome, named Clement, wrote a letter to the church at Corinth (known as *I Clement*), in which he quotes from Hebrews. This shows that Hebrews was known in Rome, and suggests that it was originally sent there. There is the greeting in Hebrews 13: 24 'from our

Italian friends', which might (but need not) be greetings from Italian Christians to their fellow-countrymen in Rome. The subject of Hebrews also fits Rome, where there was a Jewish community (Acts 18: 2 and 28: 17) and a Christian one (Acts 28: 15) to which Paul wrote a letter largely about Judaism and Christianity (the Letter to the Romans). This theory rests on slight but good evidence.

(*b*) *The Church at Colossae.* Hebrews deals with some of the same questions as Paul's Letter to the Colossians—for instance, the angels, the sovereignty of Christ, certain Jewish observances. It could therefore be addressed to the same readers, the Christians at Colossae, Laodicea, and Hierapolis (Col. 1: 2 and 4: 13). This theory rests on reasonable deduction from the two letters, but the questions they both deal with could have arisen in more than one place, and the parallels are not so close as to demand the same destination for both letters.

(*c*) *A group influenced by Essene Judaism.* Not a theory of place, but a special theory about the sort of Judaism involved. The Essenes were a movement within Judaism (see *Understanding the New Testament* in this series, pp. 31 ff.) to which, according to most scholars, belonged the community at Qumran which produced the Dead Sea Scrolls. The Scrolls reflect the community's belief that it was the true Israel in the desert, its repudiation of the Jerusalem sacrifices, its belief in the angels, and its expectation of two Messiahs, a priestly and a princely one. All these themes correspond to parts of Hebrews, which might therefore have been written to counteract the influence of Essene Judaism.

This theory presents two main difficulties: (i) The themes common to Hebrews and the Scrolls are not exclusively Essene, but are found in other Jewish writings of the period. (ii) Certain themes prominent in the Scrolls—for example, their fanatical devotion to the Jewish Law—have no corresponding treatment in Hebrews. It therefore seems unlikely that Hebrews was directed against Essenism in particular.

7

None of these theories, then, is more than a possibility. We must remember how limited is our knowledge of Christianity and Judaism in the first century A.D. The letter could have been written to some church otherwise unknown to us, facing a crisis for which we have no other evidence. The argument from the contents of Hebrews is precarious, because the letter, while it certainly tells us about its writer's mind, may not tell us much of the mind of its readers. The writer probably put things in a way that he hoped would appeal to them, but whether he succeeded we cannot know. So, for example, his idea that Christians are like the Israelites in the desert does not prove that his readers were familiar with this theme (perhaps from Essene propaganda), but only that that he himself was (perhaps from a knowledge of Essene thought, but perhaps from elsewhere).

It seems best, in view of the lack of compelling evidence, to conclude that Hebrews was written to a community we cannot identify.

THE DATE OF THE LETTER

Since Hebrews is quoted by Clement of Rome in about A.D. 95, the latest date for its writing may be set at about A.D. 90.

The earliest date is harder to fix. The crucifixion of Jesus occurred between A.D. 30 and 33: it is reasonable to allow at least ten years for the development of such a mature theology as our writer's, and so the earliest date can be set at about A.D. 40.

There are two possibilities of narrowing this range of fifty years between A.D. 40 and 90:

(*a*) *Timothy*. In 13: 23 the writer says 'our friend Timothy' is released. This may be the Timothy whom Paul met at Lystra, and who became his companion (Acts 16: 1) in about A.D. 50. Our writer's words suggest that he is mentioning a well-known Christian, such as Timothy would have become after his association with Paul. This narrows the range of dates to A.D. 50–90.

(b) *The Fall of Jerusalem.* Whether or not this event was the cause of Hebrews, it may help in dating it. One of the writer's main points is that Jesus' sacrifice has rendered the Jewish sacrifices obsolete. Now it is true that he refers, not to contemporary Judaism, but to the contents of the Old Testament: but, if he was writing after the end of the Temple sacrifices in A.D. 70, it seems strange that he never mentions that event, which would give his argument such a strong support—'God has shown that the Jewish sacrifices are superseded, by allowing them to be ended.' For this reason many, including the present commentator, think that the letter must date from before A.D. 70. But there are two other possibilities: (i) Supposing the letter was written at the very time of the Fall (see p. 5, second paragraph), its date would be A.D. 70 or 71. (ii) It may be a good deal later than the Fall of Jerusalem, late enough for the writer and his readers to ignore the event altogether. But since it cannot be later than A.D. 90, only twenty years after, this seems unlikely.

WHO WROTE THE LETTER?

We will consider the three most important of the many answers that have been given to this question.

(a) *Barnabas.* The writer Tertullian, in his *De Pudicitia* (*On Modesty*), chapter 20, refers to this letter with the words 'there exists a letter of Barnabas to the Hebrews'. He is writing in about A.D. 220, and he attributes the letter to Barnabas as though this were an accepted fact. He means the Barnabas of Acts 4: 36, a Cypriot convert who became a fellow-missionary of Paul (Acts 13–15). Barnabas was a Levite, i.e. one of the Temple officials ranking next below the priests, and could have written the letter, with its knowledge of the sacrificial system. He was also prominent enough as a Christian to have written such an authoritative letter as

Hebrews. But a second-century 'Letter of Barnabas' exists, which is superficially similar to Hebrews: and it seems likely that our letter was attributed to Barnabas because of this similarity. Also, other writers of Tertullian's time show no knowledge of this attribution (see next paragraph).

(b) *Paul*. This was the traditional view from the fifth to the nineteenth century. It appears first in the writings of the two Christian scholars of Alexandria, Clement (*c.* 150–*c.* 215) and Origen (*c.* 185–*c.* 254), though their words survive only as quotations in Eusebius' *History of the Church*, book VI, chapters 14 and 25 respectively (dated about A.D. 311). Clement says that Paul wrote the letter in Hebrew and that Luke translated it into Greek. Origen says that 'the thoughts are the thoughts of the apostle' but that the writer was someone else recalling Paul's teaching. Who this writer was, says Origen, 'only God knows for certain', though current opinion in Origen's time suggests either Clement of Rome or 'Luke who wrote the Gospel and Acts'. Clement and Origen are important because they were careful scholars, and show that there was no certainty at all about the authorship. But Paul's authorship, which they suggest, became the accepted view in the Eastern Church, and (with doubts on the part of such scholars as Jerome, Augustine, and Luther) in the West also. It was thus incorporated in the Authorized (King James) Version of 1611, where the letter is called 'The Epistle of Paul the Apostle to the Hebrews'. This led to its general acceptance in English-speaking countries till modern times.

It would be very unusual to find a modern scholar holding this view, for there are no positive reasons for it, and strong reasons against it. The style of Hebrews is quite different from Paul's in Romans and Corinthians, as we can tell even in an English translation. Its thought differs from Paul's in several ways: 'faith' has a different sense, the resurrection is hardly mentioned, and there is nothing of Paul's doctrine of Christians being united 'in Christ' (e.g. Gal. 3:28), even when this would be a supremely relevant doctrine for our writer's purpose.

(c) *Apollos*. It was Luther who first suggested Apollos, the Jewish convert from Alexandria who became another of Paul's colleagues (Acts 18: 24 ff.). Many modern scholars hold this view. Its strong point is that what we are told of Apollos in Acts fits our writer so well: he was 'a Jew...an Alexandrian by birth', and an 'eloquent [N.E.B. footnote 'learned'] man, powerful in his use of the scriptures'. As we shall see, our writer is a representative of Alexandrian Judaism, and a powerful user of the Old Testament. Apollos, like Barnabas, was prominent enough to write such an authoritative letter. But it seems strange that Clement and Origen, who spent most of their lives working as theologians in Alexandria, should say nothing of Apollos.

It is not, of course, necessary to identify the writer, illuminating as this might be. If we wish to choose a name, Apollos is the best. But many of the New Testament books are thought to be by writers now unknown; the early Church seems to have contained several great writers whose names are lost, and our writer may be one of them. It is best to leave the question open.

HOW THE WRITER THOUGHT

The identity of our writer is less important than the way his mind worked. For this he has left us the solid evidence of the letter itself. A writer's way of thinking is due to his education, his reading, his intellectual surroundings, and so on—and to his own originality. We have enough of the writings of the ancient world to be able to classify various schools of thought with some precision, though it is easy to be more precise than the evidence allows, and to forget how much has probably left no literary traces. Hebrews certainly shows the marks of three intellectual influences: Christianity, Judaism, and Platonism.

(a) *Christianity*. This is so obvious that we need to be reminded of it. The writer has a background of Christian belief and practice (see e.g. 6: 1–5), and is very conscious of

having received the gospel from an earlier generation of
Christian preachers (2: 3). On this general Christian tradition
he has no doubt exercised his own powers of thought: he is
one of the great thinkers who mould Christian thought for
all who come after them. The result is a profound and co-
herent understanding of the Christian faith and life.

(*b*) *Judaism.* All the early Christians were inheritors of
Jewish thought, and this is pre-eminently true of our writer.
His very subject is the relationship of Judaism to Christianity:
he uses the Jewish scriptures with knowledge and understanding: he reveres the heroes of Judaism as examples to his
readers of the faith they need: his understanding of Christianity is by means of Jewish ideas and images. There can
be little doubt that he was a Jew.

Judaism in the first century A.D. had developed consid-
erably beyond what most of the Old Testament books contain. The books we call 'Apocrypha' were written later than
the Old Testament, and so were other works which survive, such as the Dead Sea Scrolls and a number of books
usually called 'Pseudepigrapha' ('falsely titled') because they
bear the names of men dead long before they were written
(e.g. the *Assumption of Moses*). These all show us that by our
writer's time Judaism contained many varieties of thought,
some of which had important influence on the early Christians. This varied Judaism of the period after the writing of the
Old Testament books is usually termed 'Late Judaism'.

One of the varieties was 'Hellenistic Judaism'—Judaism
affected by Greek ideas, centred in Alexandria, where many
Jews had lived since the third century B.C. and had become
users of the Greek language and explorers of Greek thought.
Here was made the Greek translation of the Old Testament,
called the 'Septuagint' because it was believed that seventy
men had translated it (Latin *septuaginta*: seventy). Here lived
Philo, a Jewish philosopher (*c.* 20 B.C. to *c.* A.D. 50), who
interpreted Judaism in terms of the philosophy of Plato, and
whose work our writer knew.

(c) *Platonism*. Plato, the great Athenian philosopher of the fourth century B.C., taught that earthly things, which are passing and comparatively unreal, are derived from eternal realities in the heavenly world. The contrast between the invisible realities and their earthly 'copies' passed into Greek thought generally, and into Hellenistic Judaism: it is what is usually meant by the term 'Platonism'. It often went with the idea that the material, historical, world was of little value, and that salvation consisted in the soul's escape from the prison of the body.

Our writer makes a similar contrast between the earthly tent, 'which is only a copy and shadow of the heavenly' (8: 5), and heaven, 'the real sanctuary, the tent pitched by the Lord and not by man' (8: 2). The same contrast appears in 9: 11, 9: 23, and 10: 1. But there are significant differences between Hebrews and Platonism as generally understood. Our writer does not undervalue this world and its history, nor suggest that there is anything bad or even regrettable in the physical: indeed, he makes much of the Son of God's entry into the world and into human existence.

The real contrast in Hebrews is a threefold one: (i) between the Old Covenant and the New (a chronological contrast); (ii) between the Jewish sacrifices and that of Jesus (a contrast of outward and inward); and (iii) between the earthly tent and heaven. This last is expressed in Platonistic language, but its real basis is the Hebrew contrast of the creator God and the created world. Even in the second contrast, Jesus' sacrifice, though fundamentally his inward obedience, is effected by the outward event of his death. And even Jesus' presence in heaven in (iii) depends on his preceding, earthly, life and death.

Hebrews is a statement of the Christian gospel in terms of Judaism, a Judaism coloured by Hellenistic and even Platonistic ideas, and based on the Septuagint.

THE LANGUAGE OF THE LETTER

Like all the New Testament books, Hebrews was written in Greek, and the Old Testament quotations are from the Septuagint. There is no ground for Clement of Alexandria's statement that it was written first in Hebrew. The Greek is fluent and literary, with no trace of having been translated from another language. The use of the Septuagint provides the strongest proof. The Septuagint, though based on the Hebrew Old Testament, has in many passages a different meaning from the Hebrew. Our writer bases some of his arguments on such passages, and must therefore have used the Septuagint when he composed the letter: if he had used the Hebrew text these arguments would be impossible (see the note on 2: 7, p. 27). And if he used the Greek Old Testament, it is inconceivable that he should have been writing in Hebrew.

THE FORM OF THE LETTER

In this commentary the letter is divided into sections and subsections, with headings. This sort of tabulated analysis cannot do justice to a work like Hebrews, whose argument is complex, and whose form is dictated by the argument and indicated by verbal links and echoes of considerable subtlety: but it is useful as an introduction and for reference. Here are three analyses of different types, which should be first studied separately and then interrelated.

(a) Analysis by Sections

An adequate analysis into large sections is possible, because there are certain main turning-points in the argument of Hebrews. The turning-points, however, occur within paragraphs, so that commentators do not agree on the precise limits of the main sections. In Hebrews the main turning-points occur in the paragraphs 4: 14–16 and 10: 19–39, and the N.E.B. accordingly puts its three headings before chapters 1, 5, and 11. These headings are *Christ Divine and Human, The Shadow and the Real,* and *A Call to Faith.*

These are vivid and memorable headings, but their limitations should be noticed: (i) They suggest that the first two sections are doctrinal and the third practical, whereas doctrine and practical exhortation alternate all through the letter. (ii) The first heading really applies to chapters 1–3 : 6; the subject of chapters 1–4 is the superiority of Christ to the angels and to Moses, and an alternative heading might be *Christ the True Word of God.* (iii) The second heading does justice to the prominence of the contrasts in chapters 5–10, but misses the positive content, which could be expressed as *Christ the True Way to God.*

(b) *Analysis by Types of Discourse*

Throughout the letter the writer alternates between two types of discourse—doctrinal exposition and practical exhortation. The latter arises from the former, but the former is there for the sake of the latter. Paul in his letters usually puts all the doctrine first (e.g. Romans 1 — 11) and all the exhortation second (Romans 12 — 16). Our writer alternates throughout: and the alternation is for the most part so clearly marked that if the doctrinal passages are read continuously, and the exhortations omitted, the main argument displays its underlying continuity and coherence. The following table analyses the letter in this way.

Doctrine	*Exhortation*
1: 1–14	2: 1–4
2: 5 — 3: 6	3: 7 — 4: 13
4: 14 — 5: 10	5: 11 — 6: 20
7: 1 — 10: 22	10: 23–39
11: 1 — 12: 2	12: 3–17
12: 18–29	13: 1–25

(c) Analysis by Main Themes

This does most justice to the overlapping of the writer's three main ideas: (i) *Christ's supremacy as God's word to man.* This is announced at the beginning, and developed by two contrasts, with the angels (1: 5–14) and with Moses (3: 1–6). (ii) *Christ's supremacy as man's way to God.* This proves to be more important than (i). It begins in 2: 5–18, develops in 4: 14 — 5: 10, and is fully expounded in chapters 7 — 10. (iii) *The need for faithfulness.* This is urged as a consequence of (i) and (ii). It appears, chiefly in its negative form of warning, in the first four sections of exhortation (see previous table), and, more positively, in chapters 11 and 12.

HOW TO USE THIS COMMENTARY

We now turn to the letter itself. The notes will concentrate on four matters: (*a*) Making clear the course of the argument and the meaning of difficult passages. (*b*) Pointing out the writer's characteristic literary methods, particularly his use of the Old Testament. (*c*) Showing where the letter sheds light on its background and circumstances. (*d*) Comparing it on important points with other New Testament writers.

The Old Testament. Hebrews refers so often to the Old Testament that we have not room to explain fully the original sense of the passages quoted or alluded to. They will be described fully enough to explain our writer's use of them. But to understand them properly it would be best to study them in the Old Testament itself.

In the notes the Old Testament is normally quoted in the Revised Version, but other translations are used when necessary. The Septuagint is occasionally quoted in the commentator's own translation so as to bring out the connection between it and the text of Hebrews.

ABBREVIATIONS

LXX   The Septuagint (the Greek version of the Old Testament)

R.V.   The Revised Version of the Bible

R.S.V.   The Revised Standard Version of the Bible

N.E.B.   New English Bible

C.T.   Commentator's Translation

N.E.B. footnote.   In the Library Edition of the N.E.B. there are a number of footnotes giving alternative renderings of certain doubtful words and passages. These footnotes are not printed in our text, but where necessary they are given in the notes, preceded by the words 'N.E.B. footnote'.

✻   ✻   ✻   ✻   ✻   ✻   ✻   ✻   ✻   ✻   ✻   ✻   ✻

Christ Divine and Human

THE SUPREMACY OF THE SON

WHEN IN FORMER TIMES God spoke to our fore- **1** fathers, he spoke in fragmentary and varied fashion through the prophets. But in this the final age he has **2** spoken to us in the Son whom he has made heir to the whole universe, and through whom he created all orders of existence: the Son who is the effulgence of God's **3** splendour and the stamp of God's very being, and sustains the universe by his word of power. When he had brought about the purgation of sins, he took his seat at the right hand of Majesty on high, raised as far above the **4** angels, as the title he has inherited is superior to theirs.

✳ This opening paragraph—one sentence in Greek—sets out the writer's claim that God has revealed himself to man in the person of his Son, and that this supersedes God's previous revelation to the Jews. The rest of the letter consists of (*a*) demonstrating the truth of this claim, and (*b*) pointing its moral—that the readers must remain faithful to the new revelation.

The contrast of old and new is pressed from the beginning. It is a contrast of (*a*) Times: *former times* and *this the final age*. (*b*) Receivers of the revelation: *our forefathers* and *us*. (*c*) Agents of the revelation: *the prophets* and *the Son*.

1. *God spoke*. God's revelation is described as speech: a metaphor characteristic of the Bible, and specially appropriate in the case of *the prophets*, whose message is often called 'the word of the Lord'. John I: I-18 calls Jesus 'the Word': our writer says that God *has spoken in the Son* (verse 2).

our forefathers are the Jews. Writer and readers are descendants of Israel. This is spiritually true of them as Christians, whether or not they are Jews by race.

in fragmentary and varied fashion. Perhaps a reference to the diversity, and in some cases fragmentariness, of the prophetic books of the Old Testament. Or an indication of the writer's view of the Old Testament, as containing words spoken by God which must be separated from their contexts and given a Christian interpretation (which is exactly what our writer does).

the prophets. The writer means all the men by whom God spoke to Israel: but he probably means the Old Testament writers particularly, both of the prophetic books and of the rest. They were the agents of God's revelation: such agents between God and man are termed mediators. The writer claims that Jesus is the perfect mediator, and contrasts him with various mediators of *former times*: here *the prophets*, in verse 4 the angels.

2. *this the final age*. The writer shares the belief of the New Testament church that Christ's coming brought in the final era of the world's history, which will end when Christ

appears 'a second time' (9: 28). Cf. Paul's 'upon us the
fulfilment of the ages has come' (1 Cor. 10: 11).

the Son. No title could better express the radical contrast
between the old mediators and the new one, and its force is
increased by its place in the sentence. The uniqueness of the
Son is now expounded in the six clauses listed below. They
are about his being (his 'person') and his activity (his 'work'):
the last two are about his work as man, by which God *has
spoken to us.*

whom he has made heir to the whole universe. The Son shares
God's ownership of and sovereignty over all things. *Has made*
refers both to God's eternal gift of this destiny to the Son,
and to his exaltation of the Son by the resurrection and
ascension, when that destiny was attained.

through whom he created all orders of existence. The Son was
God's agent in creation: cf. John's 'through him all things
came to be' (John 1: 3) and Paul's 'in him everything in
heaven and on earth was created' (Col. 1: 16). The *orders* are
the various worlds which at this period were believed to
constitute the universe.

3. *who is the effulgence of God's splendour and the stamp of
God's very being.* These two metaphors express both the near
identity of the Son with God, and his derivation from him.
The word translated *effulgence* (i.e. radiance) could equally
well be translated 'reflection'. The Son radiates or reflects
God's splendour, i.e. what he is seen and known to be. *God's
very being* is what God is in himself: of this the Son is *the
stamp*—literally, the impression made by a stamp or seal, and
so the replica or mirror-image.

and sustains the universe by his word of power. The Son keeps
the universe in being: his powerful word, like a word of
command, imposes his will upon it. Note that here he is not
called God's agent, but himself wields divine power. In the
English this clause is divided from the next, but really the
two belong together, and thus link the universal and the
earthly work of the Son.

When he had brought about the purgation of sins. This one statement summarizes the achievement of the Son as man on earth. Only later does the author explain how it was done, and contrast it with the old revelation's failure to deal with sins.

purgation: cleansing, as though sin were a physical uncleanness. The idea is connected with sacrificial actions in the Old Testament, e.g. 'from all your sins shall ye be clean before the Lord', Lev. 16. 30.

he took his seat at the right hand of Majesty on high. The imagery of enthronement comes from Psalm 110: 1, 'The Lord saith unto my lord, "Sit thou at my right hand."' The Son, both divine and human, shares God's sovereignty: he has attained his appointed destiny. *Majesty* is one of the various words used by the Jews at this period to avoid, for the sake of reverence, the use of God's name.

4. This verse is a turning-point in the argument. It arises out of the previous words about the Son's enthronement in heaven, and states a contrast between him and the angels. He is *above* them, as is shown by the fact that his *title* is *superior to theirs*. This statement then becomes the subject of the next section of the letter (1: 5 — 2: 4) and the point of departure of the following one (2: 5–18).

the title: literally 'the name'. Verse 5 suggests that the name is '*Son*': but 'name' means in general 'rank' or 'status', and this is the writer's real point.

Why are the angels so prominent? The answer is not clearly given till 2: 2, where the Jewish Law is called 'the word spoken through angels'. The writer wants to show that the New Covenant has replaced the Old: he therefore argues that Jesus, the bringer of the New, is greater than the bringers of the Old. The angels are the first of these, and the highest, since they are God's heavenly messengers: so they are dealt with first. As we shall see, the next is Moses, and the writer will argue that Jesus is greater than he.

A further answer is sometimes suggested: that the readers of this letter gave particular prominence in their religious

teaching to the angels. This is true of the Qumran sect (see
p. 7): but it is true of all the Judaism of this period save that
of the Sadducees (see Acts 23: 8). The reasons given above are
sufficient. ✳

THE SON GREATER THAN THE ANGELS

For God never said to any angel, 'Thou art my Son; to-   5
day I have begotten thee', or again, 'I will be father to
him, and he shall be my son.' Again, when he presents the   6
first-born to the world, he says, 'Let all the angels of God
pay him homage.' Of the angels he says,   7

  'He who makes his angels winds,
    And his ministers a fiery flame';

but of the Son,   8

  'Thy throne, O God, is for ever and ever,
    And the sceptre of justice is the sceptre of his kingdom.
    Thou hast loved right and hated wrong;   9
    Therefore, O God, thy God has set thee above thy
      fellows,
  By anointing with the oil of exultation.'

And again,   10

  'By thee, Lord, were earth's foundations laid of old,
    And the heavens are the work of thy hands.
    They shall pass away, but thou endurest;   11
    Like clothes they shall all grow old;
    Thou shalt fold them up like a cloak;   12
    Yes, they shall be changed like any garment.
  But thou art the same, and thy years shall have no end.'

To which of the angels has he ever said, 'Sit at my right   13

14 hand until I make thy enemies thy footstool'? What are they all but ministrant spirits sent out to serve, for the sake of those who are to inherit salvation?

✴ This section is an argument from scripture, to support the statement made in verse 4. Two things here are typical of the writer: (*a*) stating a case first and arguing it afterwards, (*b*) the way he uses scripture to support the argument.

The argument can be set out thus: (i) Verses 5, 6. God calls him Son, and commands the angels to worship him. (ii) Verses 7–12. The angels are servants, but the Son is king, creator, eternal. (iii) Verses 13, 14. The Son is seated at God's right hand, but the angels are sent out as servants.

5. *God...said.* All the Old Testament quotations here are ascribed to God. Our writer sometimes ascribes O.T. quotations to the Holy Spirit or the Son, but in all cases he assumes divine authorship of the scriptures. In this he is like all the Jewish and Christian writers of his time: but they combine this apparently rigid view of scripture with great liberty in interpreting it to show what they think is the real meaning.

The quotations are from Ps. 2: 7 and 2 Sam. 7: 14. Originally they are God's words to the Israelite king and about King Solomon respectively. The king of Israel was regarded as God's son in a special way, and many of the words about him were later applied to the Messiah whom the Jews awaited. Our writer believes that Jesus is the Messiah, and applies these words to him, thus arguing that God declares him to be his Son.

6. The quotation is from the Septuagint (LXX) version of Deut. 32: 43. Originally it is part of the 'Song of Moses', and exhorts the angels to pay homage to God himself: our writer interprets it as God's command that the angels should *pay homage* to the Son, and thus as a sign that he is higher than they.

when he presents the first-born to the world. Often taken as a reference to the angels' song at Christ's birth into this world, Luke 2: 13. But *the world* probably means the 'world to come' (2: 5), and this makes it a reference to Christ's entry into

heaven (1: 3 and 4). The context supports the latter interpretation.

7. Quotation: Ps. 104: 4. Originally a statement about
God: 'he who makes winds his angels [i.e. messengers], and the
fiery flames his servants [ministers]' (C.T.). Our writer inverts
the meaning—perhaps following the writer of 2 Esdras 8: 22,
who does the same—so that it means that the angels do
God's tasks in the world of nature. They are God's servants.

8–9. But the Son is enthroned as God. Quotation: Ps. 45:
6, 7, originally the Psalmist addressing the king of Israel at
an enthronement. Our writer's application: God addressing
his Son at his enthronement in heaven. The result is that the
Son is explicitly addressed as God. This is remarkable in the
New Testament, whose writers usually imply as much but
do not state it. (The later doctrines of the Trinity are deliberate
intellectual formulations arising from such New Testament
ideas as this.)

thou hast loved right and hated wrong. For our writer, a
reference to Christ's sinless human life which is the cause of
his exaltation.

anointing with the oil of exultation. The Israelite king was
anointed (Greek *christos*, Hebrew *messiah*) with oil. The phrase
of exultation is a Hebraic way of referring to the joyfulness of
the occasion.

10–12. Further, the Son is the eternal creator. Quotation:
Ps. 102: 25–27, the Psalmist addressing God. Application: God
addressing the Son. The first case of words directed originally
to God himself being re-directed to the Son. The result here
is that the Son is made the creator (verse 10) and eternal
(verses, 11, 12): these ideas are stated in 1: 2, though there
the distinction between God and Son is explicit.

13–14. The Son is at God's *right hand*, but the angels are
ministrant spirits. A more explicit version of the argument of
verses 7–9.

ministrant and *serve* are related words in the Greek.

those who are to inherit salvation: Christians. Our writer sees *salvation* as their future entry into heaven at Christ's second coming or Parousia: see the note on 9: 28.

The idea that the angels are sent *for the sake of* men is reflected in many biblical stories: Daniel tells the king that God sent his angels and shut the lions' mouths (Dan 6: 22), and Peter is released from prison by an angel in Acts 12: 7.

This is a convenient place to notice how the writer has used the Old Testament: (*a*) He regards its words as uttered by God, whoever speaks them in their original context. They therefore have divine authority. (*b*) He alters the person who is originally addressed or referred to, in order to apply the words to Christ (in the above cases) or to Christians (see 3: 7) or to some aspect of the Christian covenant (see 8: 8). (*c*) But the changes he makes are consistent, and depend on his belief that the Christian gospel fulfils the Jewish faith. Thus, what he applies to Christ was originally about such persons as the king of Israel, the Messiah, David (the psalmist), or God: all of whom he believes Jesus to fulfil or to be. Likewise what he applies to Christians turns out to have been written of Israel, whose true descendants he believes the Christians to be. ✶

A FIRST WARNING

2 Thus we are bound to pay all the more heed to what we
2 have been told, for fear of drifting from our course. For if the word spoken through angels had such force that any transgression or disobedience met with due retri-
3 bution, what escape can there be for us if we ignore a deliverance so great? For this deliverance was first announced through the lips of the Lord himself; those
4 who heard him confirmed it to us, and God added his testimony by signs, by miracles, by manifold works of power, and by distributing the gifts of the Holy Spirit at his own will.

✻ The writer's pastoral purpose is here shown for the first time. He draws a practical conclusion from the previous argument, and does so in a characteristic way which we shall encounter again. The angels brought a law, and disobeying the law brought due punishment (2: 2). Jesus, greater than the angels, brought a greater thing: neglecting it will bring a greater punishment. This is an example of arguing *a fortiori* (from a stronger premiss).

1. *what we have been told*: the Christian gospel, described in verses 3, 4.

drifting from our course. The first hint of what the writer fears his readers will do, or have begun to do. It gives no indication what sort of failure in the Christian life is meant: but it is characteristic of the writer to think of the Christian life as a *course*, or journey.

2. *the word spoken through angels*: the Jewish Law. In 'Late Judaism' (i.e. Judaism from about 300 B.C. to A.D. 100) it was believed that Moses received the Law, not from God directly, but through angels. Paul mentions this idea in Gal. 3:19; 'It was promulgated through angels, and there was an intermediary' (i.e. Moses).

3. *a deliverance so great.* A reference back to *salvation* in 1: 14 (the same Greek word). Its greatness is expounded in verse 4.

announced through the lips of the Lord. A reference to Jesus' own preaching of the 'Gospel of God' (Mark 1: 14) during his ministry. The first of the writer's many references to Jesus' earthly life (see p. 139).

those who heard him: the disciples of Jesus during his life, and perhaps the apostles in particular. Compare Acts 1: 21, 'those who bore us company all the while we had the Lord Jesus with us'.

confirmed it to us: transmitted it so as to have convincing effect. The writer and his readers cannot, then, be apostles or disciples of Jesus. Barnabas and Apollos could have written this, but not Paul.

4. Compare this verse with Mark 16: 20, 'the Lord worked with them and confirmed their words by the miracles that followed.' Both verses are about the preaching of the apostles after Jesus' ascension: the idea is that the miraculous events that accompanied the preaching of the gospel showed that it must be true.

the gifts of the Holy Spirit: the various functions of members of the church, and the power to do them. Our writer does not say much about the Holy Spirit, but what he does say echoes the general thought of the New Testament writers. Compare Paul in 1 Cor. 12: 1–13, especially verse 4, 'There are varieties of gifts, but the same Spirit.' ✻

THE MAN GREATER THAN THE ANGELS

5 For it is not to angels that he has subjected the world to
6 come, which is our theme. But there is somewhere a solemn assurance which runs:

'What is man, that thou rememberest him,
  Or the son of man, that thou hast regard to him?
7   Thou didst make him for a short while lower than the
        angels;
    Thou didst crown him with glory and honour;
8   Thou didst put all things in subjection beneath his feet.'

For in subjecting all things to him, he left nothing that is not subject. But in fact we do not yet see all things in
9 subjection to man. In Jesus, however, we do see one who for a short while was made lower than the angels, crowned now with glory and honour because he suffered death, so that, by God's gracious will, in tasting death he should stand for us all.

✻ A new line of argument begins here. The writer has argued that the Son is higher than the angels because of his divinity and exaltation. Now he argues that God planned that the universe should be ruled by man, not by angels: and that Jesus fulfils that plan.

5. This verse picks up the argument from 1: 14, after the intervening warning.

the world to come: the heavenly world, which in a sense is the *theme* of the whole letter.

6. The writer is vague about the source of his quotation, but his use of it follows the pattern discussed previously. Quotation: Ps. 8: 4–6, about man as God's ruler over the subhuman creatures in this present world. Application: Jesus is God's ruler over all creatures in the *world to come*.

man...the son of man. The first two lines of the quotation are parallel, so that these expressions mean the same.

7. *for a short while lower than the angels.* The Hebrew says 'little lower than God', the LXX 'little lower than the angels'. The Greek for 'little lower' can be understood in a temporal sense, and our writer takes it in this way—*for a short while lower.*

8. The writer omits the first half of Ps. 8: 6, 'Thou madest him to have dominion over the works of thy hands', because it emphasizes man's rule over this material world: and he wants to apply the Psalm to Jesus' rule over the world to come. That is why he picks out *all things* and stresses its inclusiveness: he takes *all things* to include the angels.

But in fact... The Psalm is about man's universal rule: but this is clearly *not yet* true of man in general. Therefore, argues the writer, the psalm must be about Jesus, who fulfils it exactly. Verse 9 applies it to him in detail.

9. *In Jesus.* This is the first use of the Son's human name, and comes fitly at the point where the writer first stresses the Son's humanity.

for a short while. We now see why the writer gives the phrase this sense. Originally it meant that man was lower than the angels but ruler of the created world: the writer makes it mean that the man Jesus was *lower than the angels* only during his earthly life (*a short while*), after which (*now*) he is *crowned with glory and honour*, i.e. he rules over all things, including the angels.

because he suffered death. An explanation from Christian belief, inserted to make the words of the Psalm apply to Jesus, whose exaltation was the reward of his death. The next words begin to explain why his death was so important.

so that...in tasting death he should stand for us all. Literally 'so that he should taste death on behalf of every man': Christ's death in some way benefits all men. This will be explored more fully later in the letter, in chapters 9 and 10. But the writer here echoes an idea present in Late Judaism, in Jesus' teaching, and in the gospel of the New Testament church, that a righteous person's suffering somehow makes reparation for his people's sins. For the early church Jesus was the the righteous person who had thus benefited all men.

So far the writer has been concerned with mediators of God's word to men: but at this point he begins to speak of mediation in the opposite direction, from man to God. It is his second, and greater, main theme (see p. 16). ✲

MAN NEEDS TO BE SAVED BY A MAN

10 It was clearly fitting that God for whom and through whom all things exist should, in bringing many sons to glory, make the leader who delivers them perfect through
11 sufferings. For a consecrating priest and those whom he consecrates are all of one stock; and that is why the Son
12 does not shrink from calling men his brothers, when he says, 'I will proclaim thy name to my brothers; in full
13 assembly I will sing thy praise'; and again, 'I will keep my trust fixed on him'; and again, 'Here am I, and the

children whom God has given me.' The children of a 14
family share the same flesh and blood; and so he too shared
ours, so that through death he might break the power of
him who had death at his command, that is, the devil;
and might liberate those who, through fear of death, had 15
all their lifetime been in servitude. It is not angels, mark 16
you, that he takes to himself, but the sons of Abraham.
And therefore he had to be made like these brothers of 17
his in every way, so that he might be merciful and
faithful as their high priest before God, to expiate the
sins of the people. For since he himself has passed through 18
the test of suffering, he is able to help those who are
meeting their test now.

* Now comes an explanation of the inner necessity of what
has just been asserted. Jesus tasted death so as to 'stand for us all'
(verse 9): now we learn why we need someone to stand for
us all, and why he must be a man and not an angel.

10. *It was clearly fitting*. Another example of the writer's
way of making a statement first and arguing for it afterwards
(in verses 11 to 18).

God for whom and through whom all things exist. Almost
exactly what is said in 1: 2 *b* of the Son, who is thus put on
the same level as God.

in bringing many sons to glory. Here is God's destiny for
men, and the purpose of the Son's work: men are to enter as
sons that heavenly glory which is God's (1: 3 'splendour'),
which the Son reflects (1: 3) and, having become man, attains
after his death (2: 9).

the leader who delivers them. God's purpose is thwarted by
something that holds men captive; this is described elsewhere as sins (1: 3), or servitude (2: 15). They need a *leader
who delivers them*—a mediator who will bring them both
out of servitude and *to glory*. The writer has in mind Moses and

Joshua, who led Israel out of captivity in Egypt and into the promised land of Canaan. Jesus is the new leader for all men.

perfect through sufferings. Perfection is a prominent idea in Hebrews. It means the attainment of a person's proper end or destiny: for men this is heaven (*glory*), and death is an important, but not the only, step on the way. The Son is 'made perfect for ever' (7: 28) after his exaltation: the heroes of the Old Covenant are destined to 'reach their perfection' 'in company with us' (11: 40).

11. *A consecrating priest and those whom he consecrates.* Another way of stating God's purpose for men and describing the necessary mediator: this time in the language of holiness and priesthood. The writer has in mind the high priest of Israel, and God's purpose that Israel should be a 'holy nation' (Exod. 19: 6). The next verse applies this to the Son as the consecrating priest of men.

The noun *priest* is not in the Greek, but the N.E.B. rightly supplies it.

are all of one stock. Literally *are all of one*—possibly meaning 'of one man', i.e. Adam. A priest is always 'taken from among men' (5: 1): he could not properly represent them unless he was one of them.

the Son does not shrink. Why should he? Perhaps the writer is anticipating objections. A few might well object that it would be unfitting for the transcendent creator to become one with created men: others, holding the belief that matter is inherently evil, might object to a spiritual God taking on man's physical nature.

12, 13. Three Old Testament quotations are put on the lips of the Son:

(*a*) Ps. 22: 22. The Psalmist speaks to God of praising him among his brother Israelites. Application: the Son speaks of praising God (or possibly, preaching the gospel) among his brother men. The crucial point is that he is thus *calling men his brothers*, and the writer has thus given scriptural proof that the Son is really man. There may be a secondary point in the words *I will sing thy praise*: they may anticipate the writer's later theme of Jesus as the mediator of men's worship (8: 2; 13: 15).

(*b*) Isa. 8: 17, the prophet Isaiah speaks of trusting in God. Application: the Son's trust in God. The relevance of this is not obvious. But Hebrews is about the need for faith, and here the Son's faith is both an aspect of his humanity and an example to the readers.

(*c*) Isa. 8: 18, the prophet speaks of his children. Application: the Son speaks of men as his children. The analogy here is of parenthood, not brotherhood: but it proves the same point, the Son's humanity, and verse 14 actually alters the sense back to that of brotherhood.

14*a*. The meaning shifts here. Children *share the same flesh and blood* (i.e. their parents'): the Son *shared ours* (literally, 'took a share of ours'), i.e. entered the family, when he became man.

14*b*. *so that through death he might*. . .The Son became man in order to achieve something *through* (by means of) *death*:

(*a*) Breaking the power of the devil. Our writer shared the general belief of Jews and Christians of his time that personal evil powers existed, and were enemies to men. The devil *had death at his command* because he tempted Adam to sin, and God punished the sin by death (Gen. 3). Jesus' death broke the devil's power because it brought about the 'purgation of sins' (1: 3) and because Jesus rose from the dead, thus passing through the divine punishment and yet living again.

(*b*) Releasing men from the fear of death. Jesus' resurrection showed that death was not the end: men could thus lose their fear of it. This is a *liberation* from *servitude*. They do not escape death, but since they hope for salvation they can lose the enslaving fear of it.

The idea of Christ's death overcoming death and the devil is prominent in much Christian art and liturgy.

16–18. The Son overcomes not only death but sin. This is

explained by a return to the language of priesthood and sacrifice.

16. A reiteration of the Son's humanity, and a last contrast with the angels. They have been shown to be lower than the Son and incapable of delivering man: here the point is that the Son did not become an angel, but man.

the sons of Abraham. Either, literally, the Jews, of which nation the Son became a member: or, figuratively, Christians, who share Abraham's faith and inheritance (chapter 11).

17. This verse is the fullest summary of the argument so far; it draws together the ideas of 1: 3 and 2: 11, and brings in the term *high priest*, which proves to be central to the writer's thought. The Son had to be a man himself: this enabled him to understand men, to represent them adequately to God, and to remove their sins.

high priest. The chief priest of the Jews during the period after the Exile, and practically the head of the Jewish state. From the viewpoint of our writer, who took the Old Testament books as plain history, the high priesthood began when Aaron, Moses' brother, was made the chief priest of Israel at Mount Sinai (Exod. 28, Lev. 8). In Leviticus 1 — 16 are the instructions for the sacrifices over which Aaron was to preside, and his supreme priestly act was the annual ceremony described in Lev. 16 when he alone entered the inner sanctuary of the Tent to appear *before God, to expiate the sins of the people.*

By the time of Jesus all this took place in the Temple at Jerusalem, and the day (the tenth day of the seventh month, Lev. 16: 29) was called the Day of Atonement. But our writer refers always to the period of Israel's wanderings in the desert, and to the service of atonement which, according to the Old Testament, was performed every year even then.

expiate the sins of the people. The phrase is not a quotation, but it echoes several similar phrases in Lev. 16: e.g. 'to make atonement for the children of Israel', Lev. 16: 34.

expiate the sins: i.e. remove the obstacle that thwarts God's purpose for men. So far a variety of terms has been used for this process—'purgation of sins' (1: 3), 'suffered death, tasting death, stand for us all' (2: 9), 'leader who delivers them', perfection 'through sufferings' (2: 10), 'break the power of the devil' (2: 14), 'liberate' (2: 15), and the present verse. The picture emerges of Jesus liberating men from the power of death, sin, and the devil by his sacrificial death. Such imagery is common in the New Testament writers: compare Jesus' words reported in Mark 10: 45, 'surrender his life as a ransom for many', and in Mark 14: 24, 'my blood of the covenant, shed for many'.

18. *the test of suffering*. A new idea, of Jesus' sufferings as a test: perhaps brought in because the readers are *meeting their test now*. Hence also the emphasis on sufferings, testing, perfection, faithfulness, throughout the book. The Greek verb includes the two ideas of the inward testing that we call 'temptation' and the outward trials that test the strength of the sufferer's faith.

What was tested in Jesus? Here, probably, his faithfulness, mentioned in verse 17 and dwelt on in the next paragraph.

Note the inward element in what might seem the merely ceremonial idea of Jesus' high priesthood—he is *merciful and faithful, able to help* sufferers. Later his compassion is emphasized (5: 2).

We have seen that Jesus is called leader and priest. Chapters 3 and 4 develop the leader theme: Jesus is shown to be greater than Israel's leader Moses and to lead men to a better goal than Joshua, Moses' successor, did. Chapters 5–10 develop the priest theme: Jesus is the priest whose perfect sacrifice inaugurates the New Covenant. ✻

JESUS GREATER THAN MOSES

Therefore, brothers in the family of God, who share a **3** heavenly calling, think of the Apostle and High Priest of the religion we profess, who was faithful to God who 2

appointed him. Moses also was faithful in God's house-
3 hold; and Jesus, of whom I speak, has been deemed
worthy of greater honour than Moses, as the founder of a
4 house enjoys more honour than his household. For every
house has its founder; and the founder of all is God.
5 Moses, then, was faithful as a servitor in God's whole
household; his task was to bear witness to the words that
6 God would speak; but Christ is faithful as a son, set over
his household. And we are that household of his, if only
we are fearless and keep our hope high.

✵ 1. This verse shows another characteristic of the writer:
he alludes to points made earlier, and states briefly themes
which will be given full treatment later.

brothers in the family of God. Literally 'brothers, holy ones',
echoing 'brothers' from 2: 11, 12, 17, and 'those whom he
consecrates' from 2: 11. A telling way of addressing his
readers, since it applies to them the previous argument—
'So now, you who are yourselves Jesus' brothers, consecrated
by him...'

who share a heavenly calling. The phrase reflects the writer's
view of the Christian life as directed to a future salvation in
heaven.

the Apostle (N.E.B. footnote, *Envoy*). The word used in the
New Testament for the twelve apostles, Paul, etc., but
nowhere used for Jesus except here. The idea, however
(somebody who is sent forth), is often applied to Jesus, as
one sent from God (cf. Jesus' words in John 20: 21, 'As the
Father sent me, so I send you'). Here the word sums up our
writer's teaching about the Son coming as God's word into
the world: and so the double title *Apostle and High Priest*
sums up Jesus' double role as mediator of God's revelation
to man and of man's response to God.

The introduction of Moses in the next verse suggests the

same interpretation. Though Moses is not called 'apostle' or 'envoy', the story of his vision of God in the burning bush repeats several times the assertion that he is sent by God to Israel. As for 'high priest', Moses was reckoned to have virtually possessed the high priesthood by Philo, who influenced our writer (see p. 12). There are several stories in Exodus and Numbers of Moses' effective intercession for Israel.

the religion we profess: our religion, perhaps in contrast with Judaism.

2–6. The writer argues that Jesus is greater than Moses: (*a*) because the founder of a house is greater than a member; (*b*) because the son of a house is greater than a servant. The contrast depends verbally on the phrase *in God's household*.

Moses was uniquely great in the eyes of the Jews: hence our writer's need to show that Jesus is greater still. Moses had three great functions: (*a*) He was the leader who delivered Israel from Egypt (cf. 2: 10); (*b*) he was God's spokesman to Israel at Sinai (Exod. 19—24); (*c*) he pleaded with God for Israel when they sinned (e.g. Exod. 32: 11-14). Our writer certainly has (*a*) in mind, and possibly (*c*), but it is (*b*) that matters most: Moses, like the angels, is superseded as God's spokesman by Jesus.

2. The apparently abrupt, but in fact carefully planned, way in which Moses is introduced is typical of the writer. It depends on a loose quotation (not apparent in the N.E.B.) from Num. 12: 7, where God praises Moses with the words 'My servitor Moses is not like that; he is faithful in my whole household' (C.T.). Our writer applies 'faithful' first to Jesus (*faithful to God*), and then to Moses: with the qualification *in God's household*, which he then uses to argue that Jesus is the greater.

God's household: in Num. 12: 7, Israel. Our writer extends it in verse 6 to mean believers in Christ, regarded as the real Israel. He can thus use the word when talking either of Jesus in the present or of Moses in the past.

3. An argument from a general truth: a founder is greater than the household he founds. Moses was *in*, i.e. part of, the household.

4. We expect to read now that Jesus was the founder of the household: but the writer does not say so. Perhaps he avoids it because the plain sense of the Old Testament says nothing of it, and he would have to digress and justify such a statement. He prefers to go back to a more fundamental one, that God is the *founder of all*. He may have in mind that Jesus, as God's agent in creation, is also therefore *founder of all*, and thus plainly greater than Moses. In any case he moves on to the second, clearer, contrast.

5, 6. Num. 12: 7 is quoted more fully to include the word *servitor*. Then the writer seizes upon the two words *servitor* and *in*, and (verse 6) contrasts Jesus, the *son* set *over* the household.

5. Moses' task as a servitor was *to bear witness to the words that God would speak*; that is, to pass on God's words to Israel, chiefly in receiving the Law at Sinai, where he was the human counterpart to the angels. A contrast with Jesus who actually embodied God's words ('spoken to us in the Son', 1: 2) may be intended, though not stated.

6. *set over*: a reference to Jesus' exaltation to heaven. He is superior by both his innate sonship and his glorification.

if only ... The writer qualifies his statement *we are that household*, because he has such a strong sense that salvation is in the future. He believes that Christians already have a foretaste of salvation, but if they are unfaithful they will lose the final reality of it. ✶

A SECOND WARNING:

(*a*) GOD WILL REJECT THE FAITHLESS

'Today', therefore, as the Holy Spirit says—　　　　7

'Today if you hear his voice,
Do not grow stubborn as in those days of rebellion,　　8
At that time of testing in the desert,
Where your forefathers tried me and tested me,　　9
And saw the things I did for forty years.
And so, I was indignant with that generation　　10
And I said, Their hearts are for ever astray;
They would not discern my ways;
As I vowed in my anger, they shall never enter my rest.'　　11

See to it, brothers, that no one among you has the 12
wicked, faithless heart of a deserter from the living God;
but day by day, while that word 'Today' still sounds in 13
your ears, encourage one another, so that no one of you is
made stubborn by the wiles of sin. For we have become 14
Christ's partners if only we keep our original confidence
firm to the end.

When Scripture says, 'Today if you hear his voice, do 15
not grow stubborn as in those days of rebellion', who, I 16
ask, were those who heard and rebelled? All those, surely,
whom Moses had led out of Egypt. And with whom was 17
God indignant for forty years? With those, surely, who
had sinned, whose bodies lay where they fell in the
desert. And to whom did he vow that they should not 18
enter his rest, if not to those who had refused to believe?
We perceive that it was unbelief which prevented their 19
entering.

✲ The ominous *if only* of verse 6 leads into a full-scale warning lasting from 3: 7 to 4: 13, which tells us more clearly what the writer fears for his readers. The whole section depends on the parallel between the Israelites in the desert and Christians in this world.

The Old Testament parallel arises out of the section on Moses, the leader who delivered Israel from Egypt, and who then led them through the desert towards the promised land. According to Exodus and Numbers, the Israelites continually lost faith in God's promise of the land, and, when they arrived at its borders, refused to enter it for fear that they could not overcome its inhabitants (Num. 14). God therefore (Num. 14: 20–35) condemned them to stay in the desert forty years, so that they would die and never enter the promised land.

The readers have similarly been delivered by their leader Jesus; God has promised them a 'land', which is heaven; meanwhile they must keep faithful. If they rebel like the Israelites, God will not allow them to enter their heavenly inheritance.

7–11. The warning is based on Ps. 95: 7–11. It is important to remember how the writer views the Psalms. He believes that they are the utterance of God through David, who wrote the Psalms during his reign as king of Israel (2 Samuel 23: 1). So this Psalm was a warning from God to Israel through David, urging them not to be rebellious and lose God's reward as their ancestors had, on the notorious occasion when they refused to enter the land of Canaan (Numbers 14). Our writer takes this warning and applies it to his readers: they, too, need to recall what happened at the entrance to Canaan. He bases his argument on the Psalm's version of the incident, but also on the story in Num. 14: he allows himself to treat the two passages as complementary and to quote from both. At the same time, part of his argument depends on the chronological sequence—the actual incident first, and the Psalmist's reference to it centuries later. (It is important to be well acquainted with Num. 14 at this point.)

7. *As the Holy Spirit says*. The Jews and the Church after them believed the Scriptures (i.e. the Old Testament) to be inspired by God, and so to be the work of his Spirit. Our writer mentions the Spirit in this way here and at 10: 15, but there is no special reason for his doing so in these particular places. He simply varies his way of introducing scripture.

Today if you hear his voice: originally the Psalmist addressing his people, who are in danger of refusing to listen to God. For our writer, God's address to the readers who are in a similar danger.

8. *Do not grow stubborn*. The readers were warned of 'drifting from their course' in 2: 1. Here they are warned of the positive sin of stubborn refusal to trust God: in verse 19 he names their sin *unbelief*, i.e. unfaithfulness.

8, 9. The Psalm recalls various occasions when Israel *tried* God (i.e. tried his patience) by complaining of their hardships in the desert and losing faith in their destined goal.

9. *And saw the things I did for forty years*. The original sense of the Psalm is as follows—

> When your fathers tried me and tested me,
> Though they saw the things that I did.
> For forty years I was indignant with that generation.

Here *the things I did* means the miraculous acts by which God rescued Israel from Egypt, despite which Israel rebelled.

Our writer attaches *for forty years* to the previous sentence, and it thus becomes the duration, not of God's curse, but of Israel's rebelliousness, the obstinacy of which is thus further emphasized.

10. *that generation*. God's anger was against the generation of Israelites who left Egypt and lost faith, but not against their descendants. He delayed the entry into Canaan for forty years because that was the time it would take for *that generation* to die out, and so never to enter the land. They themselves were thus rejected finally.

11. *my rest*: i.e. the land destined by God where they would

come to rest from their desert wanderings: called in Deut. 12:
9 'the rest and the inheritance which the Lord thy God giveth
thee'. Much is built on these two words in chapter 4.

12–14. A straightforward application of the warning to the
readers. Notice how single words from the psalm are incorporated—*heart*, *Today*, *stubborn*. But at the same time the
writer's theme is brought in by the words *faithless, deserter*.

12. *faithless*. It is implied that the Israelites lacked faith,
though the psalm does not say so. This will be argued in
verses 15–19.

13. Notice how *Today* is used to give a sense of present
urgency.

encourage one another. The writer's grave warnings are
balanced by his more positive note of encouragement based
on the supremacy of Jesus and the greatness of the promised
salvation.

14. *have become Christ's partners*. Not Paul's idea of Christians as 'Christ's body, and each...a limb or organ of it'
(1 Cor. 12: 27), but the idea of sharers in a common possession.

if only. The same tone as verse 6. It betrays the writer's
fear that they will not keep their *confidence firm to the end*.

confidence. In 11: 1 the Greek word is part of the writer's
definition of 'faith'. The quality he calls faith includes belief,
confidence, hope, fidelity, perseverance, and other-worldliness:
his readers' desertion would be a failure of faith.

15–19. The writer now refers to the original subject of the
quotation, the Israelites, in order to bring out three implicit
points about their story which are closely paralleled in his
readers—they had been delivered, they sinned, they refused to
believe.

The argument may be set out as follows:

(i) (15, 16) Who heard and rebelled?	Those who had been de-livered.
(ii) (17) Who suffered God's anger?	Those who had sinned.

(iii) (18, 19)   Who did not   Those who were faithless.
          enter his rest?

The implication is that if the readers fit the second column, they fit the first too.

16. *who, I ask, were those who heard and rebelled?* The writer has just quoted the first words of the Psalm (in verse 15), and now picks out of it these words, which enable him to refer back to Num. 14: 22, where God says that the people 'have not hearkened to my voice'. In 4: 2 he will apply this to the readers, who 'have heard the good news' but are in danger of rebelling.

All those, whom Moses had led out of Egypt. That is, those who had been delivered by God. 'Who rebelled?—the very people who had been delivered'—stressing their ingratitude.

17. *those who had sinned*: a fair inference, though the word 'sin' does not occur in the quotation. 'Who was God angry with?—the people who sinned.'

whose bodies. . . an allusion to God's sentence in Num. 14: 29, 'your carcases shall fall in this wilderness'.

18. *those who had refused to believe.* Again an inference, enabling the writer to bring out the similarity with his readers' sin.

19. *We perceive that it was unbelief.* A fair definition of the Israelites' sin, as Num. 14 shows. God speaks of their unbelief when he asks Moses 'How long will they not believe in me?' (Num. 14: 11).

Verse 19 sums up the argument of this section. The writer has proved from Ps. 95 that the Israelites (*a*) sinned through faithlessness and (*b*) lost their promised rest. The latter point leads to the next section. ✻

41

A SECOND WARNING:

(*b*) THE FAITHLESS WILL LOSE HEAVEN

4 Therefore we must have before us the fear that while the promise of entering his rest remains open, one or another among you should be found to have missed his chance.

2 For indeed we have heard the good news, as they did. But in them the message they heard did no good, because they brought no admixture of faith to the hearing

3 of it. It is we, we who have become believers, who enter the rest referred to in the words, 'As I vowed in my anger, they shall never enter my rest.' Yet God's work has been

4 finished ever since the world was created; for does not Scripture somewhere speak thus of the seventh day: 'God

5 rested from his work on the seventh day'?—and once again in the passage above we read, 'They shall never

6 enter my rest.' The fact remains that someone must enter it, and since those who first heard the good news failed to

7 enter through unbelief, God fixes another day. Speaking through the lips of David after many long years, he uses the words already quoted: 'Today if you hear his voice,

8 do not grow stubborn.' If Joshua had given them rest, God would not thus have spoken of another day after

9 that. Therefore, a sabbath rest still awaits the people of

10 God; for anyone who enters God's rest, rests from his

11 own work as God did from his. Let us then make every effort to enter that rest, so that no one may fall by following this evil example of unbelief.

✶ This section applies verse 3: 19 to the readers: let them not be 'prevented from entering' by their 'unbelief'. The main argument is in verses 1–3 a (ending at '... *enter my rest*'), and verse 11, the latter corresponding exactly with 3: 19.

Verses 3 b to 10 are a digression, arguing that the *rest* in Psalm 95 means not the promised land, which Israel did finally enter, but heaven, which the readers have still to attain.

1. A return to the warning note. The parallel adduced in 3: 15–19 shows that some among the readers may be in danger of losing their entry into God's rest.

But the readers can only be warned against losing God's rest if it is still in the future. Hence the statement that the *promise of entering his rest remains open*: the entry into his rest still lies before them, to be gained or lost. They are still in the desert, as it were.

should be found: i.e. in the future, when he approaches the rest. The writer is thinking of the day of judgement.

2. This picks up 3: 16, 'those who heard and rebelled.' A further parallel: the readers have heard the good news (the Christian gospel), as the Israelites did (probably meaning God's promise of the land of Canaan, Exod. 3: 17).

But in them...Now a contrast: the readers have believed, but the Israelites did not.

the message they heard did no good. They did not benefit from the *message* (*the good news*), but failed to enter the Rest.

because they brought no admixture of faith. The exact meaning is obscure, but the main point is clear enough: they lacked faith in God's promise.

3 a. But those *who have become believers*, i.e. Christians, do receive the benefit of the good news, and *enter the rest* (the present tense is not significant here: the sense is 'are those who will enter the rest').

3 b–10. The writer in these verses gives a proof of his statement in 4: 1 that *the promise of entering his rest remains open*. In order to do so he must argue that in Psalm 95 the *rest* does not mean the promised land, but heaven. His argument is particularly involved, and its outline is best given before commenting on the details. It depends on the idea that

Psalm 95 gives God's words to Israel in the time of David, centuries after the rejection of the first generation of Israelites in the desert.

(i) God calls it *my rest*. This means the rest he himself enjoys. It must therefore be the rest which he began when the work of creation was finished: it is therefore the life of heaven.

(ii) David's words to Israel in Ps. 95 are a warning, but they must imply the corresponding promise, 'Today if you hear his voice, and believe him, you shall enter his rest.' The Psalm is therefore an offer, a renewed promise of God's rest, to the Israel of David's time.

(iii) This rest cannot be Canaan, because (*i*) David is speaking of it as still in the future, and Canaan was for him in the past; (*ii*) Joshua's generation did in fact enter Canaan, so it must be something else which God offers to David's generation centuries later.

Conclusion: the Rest is heaven, which lies before the readers either to enter by faith or lose by *unbelief*.

We now look at the details.

3*b*. *Yet God's work has been finished*. This means 'Yet God has been at rest': it shows that the writer has taken *my rest* to mean 'the rest I enjoy'. (In fact the Psalm meant 'the rest I bestow': our writer has either not seen this or chosen to take it in the other sense.)

3, 4. These verses mean 'We Christians are to enter God's rest: yet he has been resting since the creation: so it is heaven that we enter.'

4. Part of Gen. 2: 2 is quoted to support 3*b*. The whole verse is, however, assumed—'And on the seventh day God finished his work which he had made; and he rested on the seventh day from all his work which he had made.' God had finished his work: so the rest he began then must have gone on ever since.

5. The repetition of Ps. 95: 11 is in order to exhibit that the two passages are speaking of the same *rest*. In the Greek the same word is used in both.

6. *The fact remains that someone must enter it.* The writer infers this from the Psalm: God's vow that the unbelieving shall not enter implies that others will. The sense of verse 6 is then: 'Someone is to enter: the original hearers did not: so God renews his offer at another time.'

6, 7. *another day.* The word *day* links the Israelites' rejection in the days of rebellion and the offer to David's generation (*Today*).

7. *Speaking...after many long years.* The point depends on David the Psalmist living centuries later than the Exodus. In 1 Kings 6: 1 the time from the Exodus to the reign of Solomon, David's son, is given as 480 years. (This figure is probably an artificial one, based on 12 generations of 40 years each.)

Paul makes a similar point in Gal. 3: 17, where he argues that since Abraham lived 430 years before Moses, God's promise has priority over his Law. Our writer uses another chronological argument in 7: 9.

8. *If Joshua had given them rest.* The objection might be made that, although the first generation were excluded, the next generation under Joshua did in fact enter Canaan. Hence this further line of argument that the Rest cannot have been Canaan because, if it had been, God could not have promised it to a later generation.

Joshua was Moses' successor as leader of Israel: he therefore led them into Canaan at the end of the forty years of wandering. The Greek version of his name, in the LXX and in Hebrews, is 'Jesus': so the verbal similarity suggests the similarity of the leader into Canaan and the leader into heaven, even while the sentence is stressing the difference. The writer does not develop this parallel at all, despite its relevance to his argument: he may not have intended it, though he cannot have failed to notice it. Or he may have intended it and preferred not to develop it.

9. The conclusion: the *rest* is still in the future for God's people, i.e. the readers. A further point is added—it is a

sabbath rest. Sabbath (Hebrew for 'rest') was the Jewish name for the seventh day: our writer uses it to evoke its associations of rest after work, and then explains it in verse 10.

10. God's rest from his work on the seventh day was, according to Gen. 2: 3, the origin of the Jewish custom of resting from work every seventh day. So to enter God's rest is to enter a rest from work. The Christian life in this world is hard work, to be followed by the eternal rest with God.

11. A summary of the whole second warning, re-echoing its two main themes, *the rest* and *unbelief*. No more will be said of *the rest*: its place is filled by other images of heaven— the tent, the sanctuary, the city.

By now it is beginning to look as if our writer is basing the entire letter on the analogy between Christians in this life and Israel in the desert. Israel had been saved from Egypt through Moses, but their life was directed to the future rest in Canaan, and meanwhile they were travelling through the desert. Christians have been saved from sin and death through Jesus, but their life, too, is essentially forward-looking, to the rest in heaven: meanwhile they travel through this life. They have the same need for faith, the same penalty for unbelief.

Further details of the analogy are brought in as the book proceeds—the tent, the sacrifices, the covenant, the future city. And the chief theme, that of the High Priest, is also part of it: for just as Aaron ministered in the tent during the years in the desert, so Jesus ministers in the heavenly sanctuary during the Christians' journey through life.

Two points should be noted here: (*a*) Though the writer describes Christianity in terms of Judaism, Christianity is for him the final reality, and Judaism the preparation, a shadow of the real. This sort of analogy is called typology, the earlier thing being the 'type' and the later the 'antitype'. (*b*) This 'desert wandering' idea is not necessarily our writer's only picture of the Christian life; it may simply be the view of it which he thinks most understandable to his readers and most suitable for their needs. ✳

THE WORD OF GOD JUDGES ITS HEARERS

For the word of God is alive and active. It cuts more 12
keenly than any two-edged sword, piercing as far as the
place where life and spirit, joints and marrow, divide. It
sifts the purposes and thoughts of the heart. There is 13
nothing in creation that can hide from him; everything
lies naked and exposed to the eyes of the One with whom
we have to reckon.

✳ The 'Second Warning' has been about God speaking in
promise and in judgement. It prompts the writer to a general
statement about the effect of God's word to man: the answer
a man makes to it exposes the deepest truth about him. But
these verses are also a fitting end to the first chapters, which
have all been about the *word of God* spoken in his Son—
greater than his word through the angels and Moses, and
therefore bringing a greater penalty if the readers lose faith
in it. Hence now the emphasis on the active judgement it
brings.

12. *The word of God.* This includes 'his voice' of warning
in Ps. 95, 'the message' the first Israelites heard, 'the words'
to which Moses bore witness (3: 5), 'the word spoken through
angels' (2: 2), his word 'through the prophets' (1: 1) and
above all 'in the Son' (1: 2).

alive and active. It has effects upon its hearers: it has no
neutrality.

two-edged sword. Perhaps a suggestion of the two possible
effects, salvation and condemnation.

life and spirit, joints and marrow. Not an indication of the
writer's ideas about human biology, but a rhetorical expression of the completeness of the divisive power of God's word.

13. What is true for man is true for the whole created
universe. A fitting return to the cosmic viewpoint of 1: 1–3.

This climax of warning is followed by an equally strong

piece of positive encouragement, in verses 14–16. The change of tone corresponds to a change of direction. Chapters 1 — 4 are mainly about God's word to man, and the necessity of obeying it; 5 — 10 are mainly about man's way to God, and the necessity of following it. So from now on the figures of the angelic and human mediators of God's word to man recede into the background, and are replaced by the figure of the High Priest, the mediator of man's access to God. ✻

JESUS GIVES US ACCESS TO GOD

14 Since therefore we have a great high priest who has passed through the heavens, Jesus the Son of God, let us
15 hold fast to the religion we profess. For ours is not a high priest unable to sympathize with our weaknesses, but one who, because of his likeness to us, has been tested
16 every way, only without sin. Let us therefore boldly approach the throne of our gracious God, where we may receive mercy and in his grace find timely help.

✻ These three verses can be regarded as the statement of the central theme of the letter, and chapters 5 — 10 as their supporting argument and development. The N.E.B. heading ' *The Shadow and the Real*' ought perhaps to have come here rather than at 5: 1.

14. The opening words resume the main argument, by echoing *high priest* from 2: 17 and 3: 1.

Notice that the *high priest* theme is all part of the analogy with Israel in the desert. Our writer regards Aaron as the first high priest, appearing annually for the people, in the tent before God, as they wander for forty years. When he writes of the three figures superseded by Jesus—the angels, Moses, the high priest—he is thinking of all three in connection with that period.

a great high priest. In the Greek *great* comes after *priest*, so that it is emphatic, and linked with the following phrases which explain his greatness: he is in heaven (not in an earthly sanctuary) and he is *Son of God* (not merely man).

who has passed through the heavens: a reference to Jesus' ascension, clarifying the sense of 'before God' in 2: 17. The first statement of the main point about Jesus as high priest—that he is already with God, representing his people.

In early Christian times, there were thought to be several *heavens* between the world and God. Paul tells how he had a vision of 'the third heaven' in 2 Cor. 12: 2.

15. This verse gives the positive reason for the readers to be faithful—the effectiveness of Christ's priesthood, due to the fact that he became man, was tested, and has an inner understanding of human weakness. A summary of 2: 10–18.

his likeness to us. The noun is not meant to convey anything less than genuine humanity.

has been tested every way. Jesus is therefore able to *sympathize* with us from his own human experience.

every way is not meant literally: it expresses the completeness of Christ's sharing of human temptation.

only without sin. The early church came with remarkable speed to believe in the sinlessness of Jesus: cf. Paul, 'Christ was innocent of sin' (2 Cor. 5: 21). Jesus does not assert it in the first three Gospels: but he shows no awareness of having sinned, and himself forgives sin. Hebrews is in line with the Gospels, in which Jesus is genuinely tempted, but does not sin.

16. The most positive exhortation so far: not simply 'hold fast' under stress, but *boldly approach* God: and not 'the One with whom we have to reckon', but *our gracious God*.

boldly approach: come into God's presence. The verb is often used in Leviticus of the priests approaching God: our writer is doubtless thinking of the high priest's approach to God in the Tent (see 6: 20 especially), and he uses the same Greek verb in 7: 25, 10: 1, 10: 22, 11: 6, and 12: 18, as well as here.

This language of coming to God to worship him derived from the actual practice of worship in the sanctuaries of

Israel (e.g. Deut. 16: 16, 'Three times in a year shall all thy males appear before the Lord thy God'). It is our writer's particular way of expressing man's fellowship with God. Not that such fellowship can be taken for granted: our writer shares the Jewish belief that God's holiness forbids sinful man to approach him (cf. Hab. 1: 13, 'Thou that art of purer eyes than to behold evil, and that canst not look on perverseness'). The Jews only approached God through the high priest: our writer argues that Christians approach him through the only true high priest, Jesus. Their boldness rests on his action as their representative.

throne of our gracious God. Literally 'throne of graciousness': cf. 'throne of Majesty' in 8: 1. Because Christ is 'at the right hand of Majesty' (1: 3) as man's high priest, man can approach God confident that he is *gracious*.

Notice the contrast between the description of God in verses 14, 15, and the emphasis in this verse upon his *mercy, grace, help*.

'*Christ Divine and Human*'. At this point it may be useful to summarize the argument of chapters 1—4 in terms of the N.E.B. heading. Christ is divine, and therefore greater than the angels (chapter 1): he is human, and therefore able to save mankind as the angels cannot (chapter 2); he is divine, and therefore greater than Moses as the leader and ruler of God's people, whom he leads not to the earthly land of rest, but the heavenly one (chapters 3 and 4). ✶

The Shadow and the Real

CHRIST'S FITNESS TO BE HIGH PRIEST

5 FOR EVERY HIGH PRIEST is taken from among men and appointed their representative before God, to 2 offer gifts and sacrifices for sins. He is able to bear

patiently with the ignorant and erring, since he too is
beset by weakness; and because of this he is bound to ₃
make sin-offerings for himself no less than for the people.
And nobody arrogates the honour to himself: he is ₄
called by God, as indeed Aaron was. So it is with Christ; ₅
he did not confer upon himself the glory of becoming
high priest: it was granted by God, who said to him,
'Thou art my Son; today I have begotten thee'; as also ₆
in another place he says, 'Thou art a priest for ever, in the
succession of Melchizedek.' In the days of his earthly life ₇
he offered up prayers and petitions, with loud cries and
tears, to God who was able to deliver him from the
grave. Because of his humble submission his prayer was
heard: son though he was, he learned obedience in the ₈
school of suffering, and, once perfected, became the ₉
source of eternal salvation for all who obey him, named by ₁₀
God high priest in the succession of Melchizedek.

✲ The writer is now launched on his main subject, Jesus'
high priesthood. He first shows Jesus' fitness for it (chapter
5); then (after a digression in ch. 6) its superiority to the
Jewish high priesthood (chapter 7); lastly the superiority of
its effects (chapters 8 — 10).

1. The writer starts from general principles and describes
what he takes to be the necessary qualifications of a high priest.
Humanity, divine appointment, and sacrifice are what enable
him to represent man before God.

gifts and sacrifices for sins. Two classes of sacrifice, embodying
its two main elements: giving to God and cleansing from sin.

2, 3. An explanation of the first qualification (*taken from
among men*, verse 1). Because he is human, he has inner experience of human weakness, and therefore an inward sympathy
with sinful men. This is signified on the Day of Atonement

by the fact that he offers a bull for his own sins before offering a goat for the sins of the people (Lev. 16: 6).

4. An explanation of the second qualification. Self-appointment would be useless, for the priest is to represent the people *before God* (verse 1), and must be acceptable to God: God therefore must call him to the priesthood.

as indeed Aaron was. Aaron, Moses' brother, was the first 'high priest': his call (Exod. 28: 1-3) was by God's words to Moses. Our writer cannot use one person's name for the high priest, because it is an office held by many in succession. In chapter 7 he refers to 'Levi' because he is thinking of the priesthood in general: here, to *Aaron*, because his subject is the high priest's calling.

5-10. *So it is with Christ.* These two qualities are now shown to be possessed by Christ. The writer takes them in reverse order.

5, 6. The divine appointment. An essential point if the readers were subject to Jewish arguments about Jesus. From the Jewish point of view the Christian claims about Jesus' divine sonship were blasphemous: hence this emphasis that his high-priesthood was conferred *by God*. Scriptural authority is produced in support. Quotations: Ps. 2: 7 and Ps. 110: 4. In both, God is the speaker, and is addressing either the Israelite king or the Messiah, the future king. Application: our writer, believing that Jesus is the Messiah, can apply both quotations directly to him. He takes them as complementary, and applies them together: the resultant meaning is that God addresses his Son and appoints him *priest for ever*.

6. *in the succession of Melchizedek.* In Gen. 14: 18-20 is the story of Abraham being met and blessed by the king of Salem (Jerusalem), whose name was Melchizedek and who is there described as 'priest of God Most High'. The name occurs only once again in the Old Testament, in Ps. 110, where God declares the king (or the Messiah) to be a priest of the same kind as Melchizedek—i.e. both king and priest. Our writer will enlarge on this in chapter 7.

The Dead Sea Scrolls show that some Jews expected two Messiahs, a princely one and a priestly one. The writer may want to show the readers that there is only one, Jesus, who combines both functions as Melchizedek did.

There sprang from Hebrews a long tradition in Christian thought and art in which Melchizedek appears as a fore-shadowing or 'type' of Christ.

7–10. The human weakness. A development of verses 2 and 3. The correspondence is not exact: Jesus' weakness is not of sin, but of suffering (shown by his *strong cries and tears*), and he offered no sin offering for himself, but *prayers and petitions*. But this is enough to give him that sympathy with the ignorant and erring which a high priest needs.

7. The reference is no doubt to Jesus' prayer in Gethsemane that God would if possible save him from death (Mark 14: 32–36).

Because of his humble submission his prayer was heard. A striking comment on the Gethsemane story. Jesus' supreme quality was *submission* to God's will, and *his prayer was heard*—not indeed by avoiding death, but by being raised out of death and named high priest.

7–9. Jesus' sufferings are described by three phrases: (a) *loud cries and tears*, the outward signs of his agony; (b) *the school of suffering*—suffering was the means by which he learned the depth and cost of obedience, even though he was already disposed to obey (*son though he was*); (c) *once perfected*—his obedience was finally tested and confirmed by death.

9, 10. God's answer to Christ's prayer. It is described, not by the events of the resurrection and ascension (as elsewhere in the New Testament) but by what those events effect: (a) He *became the source of eternal salvation.* By his entry into heaven he became the means of access to God (10: 19, 20), and thus of *salvation.* (b) He was *named by God high priest.* He became man's representative to God (5: 1). The naming is thought of as taking place at the time of his entry into heaven, when also God commanded him to 'Sit at my right hand' (1: 13).

The main argument now breaks until 7: 1, when it is resumed with another reference to Melchizedek. Meanwhile the writer issues another warning like that of 3: 12 — 4: 13. ✶

THE IMMATURITY OF THE READERS

11 About Melchizedek we have much to say, much that is difficult to explain, now that you have grown so dull of hearing.

12 For indeed, though by this time you ought to be teachers, you need someone to teach you the ABC of God's oracles over again; it has come to this, that you need

13 milk instead of solid food. Anyone who lives on milk,

14 being an infant, does not know what is right. But grown men can take solid food; their perceptions are trained by long use to discriminate between good and evil.

✶ 11, 12. The warning is preceded by a reproach not made previously, that the readers are immature Christians. Our writer regards this as a matter for blame: they need to learn the elementary lessons all over again, when by now they *ought to be teachers*.

11. *you have grown so dull* suggests a decline in their religious vitality.

12. *ABC*: literally 'the rudiments'. The N.E.B. here translates freely, but conveys the writer's idea exactly.

God's oracles: his words to men. Perhaps, more particularly, the scriptures. If the readers have forgotten even the elementary meaning of the scriptures, they will not be capable of understanding the writer's subtle interpretation of them—like his interpretation of Melchizedek, about which he has *much to say*.

13, 14. The readers lack discrimination: they ought by now to have *trained perceptions*. The writer may be thinking of the danger they are in: they would be better able to resist it if they were wiser. ✶

THE NEED FOR DEEPER UNDERSTANDING

Let us then stop discussing the rudiments of Christianity. **6**
We ought not to be laying over again the foundations of
faith in God and of repentance from the deadness of our
former ways, by instruction about cleansing rites and the 2
laying-on-of-hands, about the resurrection of the dead
and eternal judgement. Instead, let us advance towards
maturity; and so we shall, if God permits. 3

✻ In fact the writer does not return to the ABC, but proceeds to more advanced teaching (*let us advance towards
maturity*, verse 2). This is apparently a contradiction: but the
words in 5: 12 were an ironical rebuke, not a literal statement. In fact the readers need help at the point they have
arrived at, and this really requires an advance in their understanding, not a repetition of earlier lessons.

The special interest of this paragraph lies in its passing
references to various things which the writer regards as
rudiments of Christianity. For two verses, we see, not his
individual understanding of Christianity, but the background
of the ordinary Christianity of his time, which he knows and
can assume his readers will know. Compare Paul's references
to general church life in Corinthians (e.g. 1 Cor. 11: 2,
'the tradition I handed on to you').

The contrast here is not the distinction made by the
'gnostics' of the second century A.D., between ordinary
Christians who lived by faith, and gnostic ('knowing') Christians who lived by a special mystic knowledge. It is simply
the difference between the teaching and sacraments connected
with conversion to Christianity and the deeper understanding
of maturer Christians.

1, 2. The writer mentions six *rudiments*, but his Greek
syntax is ambiguous. The N.E.B. text groups them as two
foundations, i.e. *faith* and *repentance*, laid by means of *instruction*

in four particular subjects. The N.E.B. footnote offers an alternative translation, *We ought not to be laying the founda-tions over again: repentance from the deadness of our former ways and faith in God, instruction about cleansing rites*...This puts all six things under the heading of *foundations*. The differ-ence does not matter greatly: either way, the six things are concerned with the instruction given to a new convert to Christianity.

faith in God. Here *faith* is probably used in its general sense of 'belief and trust', rather than the writer's special sense ex-pounded in chapter 11. It is belief that the gospel is true—i.e. that God has saved man through Jesus Christ—and the consequent self-committal to God.

repentance from the deadness of our former ways. The negative side of *faith in God*—the repudiation of the sinful life, which was deathly by contrast with the Christian life: turning from sin as a first step in turning to God. 'Repent and believe' is the double call of Christianity according to all the New Testa-ment writers, and, according to Mark 1: 15, follows Jesus' own preaching, 'repent, and believe the Gospel'.

cleansing rites: literally 'baptisms'. The plural is striking because everywhere else in the New Testament 'baptism' is in the singular. If taken with the previous words *instruction about*, the meaning is 'instruction about the various cleansing rites and their differences'. This means, perhaps, instruction about proselyte baptism (one of the ceremonies by which Gentiles became proselytes, i.e. members of Judaism), about John the Baptist's baptism, and about Christian baptism. This would be particularly relevant to the readers' problem.

the laying-on-of-hands. In the Acts of the Apostles, and later Christian practice, baptism was followed by the laying of the apostle's or bishop's hands on the convert's head. It was a Jewish practice originally, signifying the bestowal of divine power: in Acts it is a means of bestowing the Holy Spirit (e.g. Acts 8: 17, 19: 6).

These two rites clearly accompany the beginning of the

Christian life. The last two *rudiments*, however, seem at first sight to be connected with its end, not its beginning.

the resurrection of the dead. This means the raising of the human dead at the second coming of Christ, made possible by Christ's resurrection. It is treated fully by Paul in 1 Cor. 15 and 1 Thess. 4: 13-18.

eternal judgement. A second and negative aspect of the second coming of Christ: the judgement that will finally divide the saved from the lost. (Compare Matt. 25: 31-46, John 5: 28 ff.)

The mental leap from baptism to the last judgement is not as strange as it seems. The early Christians expected the end of the world to come soon, so that baptism gave entry into the community which eagerly awaited the end. But this entry was itself the crucial change, from a life of *deadness* to a new life: the final resurrection and judgement would only finalize what had taken place in baptism. Cf. Paul's teaching on baptism in Rom. 6: 1-11, especially verse 5, 'if we have become incorporate with him in a death like his, we shall also be one with him in a resurrrection like his'. ✻

A THIRD WARNING:

DESERTERS WILL HAVE NO SECOND CHANCE

For when men have once been enlightened, when they 4 have had a taste of the heavenly gift and a share in the Holy Spirit, when they have experienced the goodness of 5 God's word and the spiritual energies of the age to come, and after all this have fallen away, it is impossible to 6 bring them again to repentance; for with their own hands they are crucifying the Son of God and making mock of his death. When the earth drinks in the rain that falls 7 upon it from time to time, and yields a useful crop to those for whom it is cultivated, it is receiving its share of blessing from God; but if it bears thorns and thistles, it is 8

worthless and God's curse hangs over it; the end of that is
9 burning. But although we speak as we do, we are convinced that you, my friends, are in the better case, and
10 this makes for your salvation. For God would not be so
unjust as to forget all that you did for love of his name,
when you rendered service to his people, as you still do.
11 But we long for every one of you to show the same eager
12 concern, until your hope is finally realized. We want you
not to become lazy, but to imitate those who, through
faith and patience, are inheriting the promises.

✲ The writer now states a principle which will reappear in
chapters 10 and 12: that if a Christian falls away he cannot
start the Christian life again. In the early Church, persecution
caused many Christians to renounce their religion, and this
act, called 'apostasy' ('standing away'), was naturally regarded
as a very grave sin. There was also the view in some parts of
the Church in the third and fourth centuries that to commit
any grave sin after baptism was to set oneself beyond God's
forgiveness. Our writer is not necessarily reflecting a view
held in the Church of his time: his view may be simply
his own, produced by his serious estimate of his readers'
plight.

4, 5. These verses summarize what Christians receive at
their initiation. The writer is probably thinking of baptism
in particular.

enlightened: a word used of the baptized, in the second
century, and probably so here. The idea that the initiate
leaves darkness and enters light is common to many religions.

a taste of the heavenly gift: i.e. the gift of eternal (heavenly)
life, which, though not fully received until the second coming
of Christ, is already *tasted* in the present world. Perhaps a
reference to the eucharist, the meal in which this life was given
to Christians.

a share in the Holy Spirit. The writer shares the belief we find in the New Testament in general, that Christians are given God's Spirit, by which he himself works in them. See the note on 6: 2, 'the laying-on-of-hands': here too that ceremony may be in mind.

the goodness of God's word. The *word* is the gospel: the Christian has *experienced* for himself that the gospel he has believed is good.

the spiritual energies of the age to come. Closely linked with the previous phrase: compare 2: 3, 4, where the gospel is accompanied by 'works of power' and 'gifts of the Holy Spirit'. The *age to come is* the heavenly life after the Parousia (p. 24), of which Christians already have a foretaste: cf. Rom. 8: 23, 'we, to whom the Spirit is given as firstfruits of the harvest to come'.

6. *and after all this have fallen away.* The words *all this* are the key to the writer's severity. The Christian has entered already upon the life of heaven, than which nothing can be greater. To fall away from this is to reject eternal life, to commit spiritual suicide: therefore the writer regards it as irrevocable.

This severity springs from the belief that in accepting or rejecting Christ men are making decisions of ultimate importance: and this belief echoes Jesus' own teaching according to all the gospels—e.g. Matt. 10: 33, 'whoever disowns me before men, I will disown him before my Father in heaven'.

it is impossible: the writer sees it as a fact. A man who falls away makes himself incapable of returning.

for…they are crucifying the Son of God. A further sign of the seriousness of falling away: it is a sin comparable with that of crucifying Christ, as though deserters did it *with their own hands.*

and making mock of his death. Jesus' death was the costly means of salvation. To fall away is to belittle not only the gift but also the cost of it.

7, 8. The principle just stated is illustrated by an agricultural analogy. It is a strained one, for it depends on the idea that the earth is morally responsible for the results of the rainfall. The fact is that our writer, in his concern for the readers, never really gets away from their actual situation: so that the analogy does not have independent validity—it is more like an allegorical story. The rain falls and the earth drinks it in: it either yields a crop or bears thorns and thistles; and it is accordingly blessed or cursed by God. Similarly the gospel was preached, and the readers accepted it: they may be faithful, or fall away, and will accordingly receive salvation or damnation.

The writer is also influenced by the story in Genesis 3, of how God cursed the earth after Adam and Eve fell. He may also be thinking of the parable in Isaiah 5: 1-7, of Israel as God's unfruitful vineyard. The destruction of unproductive plants is a theme in the teaching of several prophets, and of Jesus himself.

8. *thorns and thistles*: a quotation from Gen. 3: 18.

God's curse refers to Gen. 3: 17. The Christian who deliberately falls away incurs God's positive hostility: compare the 'two-edged sword' in 4: 12.

the end of that is burning. Fire, signifying God's final destruction of evil, is an Old Testament image, used by Jesus himself and the New Testament writers. It signifies God's action upon whatever finally opposes his will: the biblical writers believe that God will in the end thus destroy persistent evil. Notice how our writer ends his warnings on a striking and terrible note: compare 4: 12, 13, and, later, 10: 31 and 12: 29.

9-12. The warning is followed by encouragement—again compare 4: 14, 15, and 10: 32.

9. *although we speak as we do.* He has stated a general truth, and emphasized its negative side, but is *convinced* that they are on the positive side. Perhaps he is less convinced than he says, but he wishes to encourage them.

10. He instances a past case of their *service* to God's *people*: probably the events more fully described in 10: 33, 34.

11. *But we long for every one of you.* By thus contrasting the community (in verse 10) with its individual members, he can call them faithful as a body (*as you still do*, verse 10) and at the same time urge them to be faithful, *every one*.

until your hope is finally realized. A good instance of the writer's understanding of the present and future aspects of salvation.

not to become lazy. To modern ears this sounds rather a mild fault in such a context. The Greek word (translated 'dull' in 5: 11) is stronger. The writer is thinking of the apathy which kills all effort—'apathetic' might be a better translation.

Those who...are inheriting are the Christians who persevere in *faith and patience*. They became inheritors at baptism and will receive the inheritance in heaven: but even now they begin to enjoy it (see notes on 6: 4, 5).

faith and patience: the great virtues, for our writer. *Patience* is faithfulness under stress, a theme first treated in chapter 5. Both were exemplified in Jesus: both are what the readers specially require now.

the promises: God's promises to various people in the Old Testament: particularly to Abraham (see 7: 6). Our writer sees all the promises as really promises of the heavenly salvation won by Christ. Cf. his treatment of 'the promise of entering his rest', Ps. 95, in 4: 1. ✻

GOD IS FAITHFUL TO HIS PROMISES

When God made his promise to Abraham, he swore by 13
himself, because he had no one greater to swear by: 'I 14
vow that I will bless you abundantly and multiply your
descendants.' Thus it was that Abraham, after patient 15
waiting, attained the promise. Men swear by a greater 16

than themselves, and the oath provides a confirmation to
17 end all dispute; and so God, desiring to show even more
clearly to the heirs of his promise how unchanging was
18 his purpose, guaranteed it by oath. Here, then, are two
irrevocable acts in which God could not possibly play
us false, to give powerful encouragement to us, who have
claimed his protection by grasping the hope set before
19 us. That hope we hold. It is like an anchor for our lives,
an anchor safe and sure. It enters in through the veil,
20 where Jesus has entered on our behalf as forerunner,
having become a high priest for ever in the succession of
Melchizedek.

⁎ As if in contrast to human faithlessness, and as a further
encouragement to the readers, the writer now stresses God's
faithfulness. They may be doubting the reality of their
promised reward: but they need not lose faith on this account,
for God always keeps his promises.

13. The word *promises* in verse 12 turns the argument to
Abraham, the ancestor of Israel. To Abraham God promised
'I will make of thee a great nation, and I will bless thee'
(Gen. 12: 2), and later (Gen. 22: 16, 17) the promise quoted
in verse 14. Paul writes about the promises to Abraham in
Galatians 3: 13–22.

he swore by himself: referring to Gen. 22: 16, 'By myself
have I sworn, saith the Lord.'

he had no one greater to swear by. The writer thinks of an oath
as having an almost objective power: to swear by God is the
strongest oath possible.

14. Quotation: Gen. 22: 17.

15. *after patient waiting attained the promise*: at the birth
of his son Abraham began to receive the promise's fulfilment.
(In a deeper sense he did not receive it until Christ, as the
writer will say in chapter 11.) Even so, it was after many years,

so that he is an example to the readers of *patient waiting* and its reward.

16. The writer explains the point of an oath: it affirms the speaker's reliability because he promises in the sight, or by the power, of a greater than himself. (Our writer of course knows that men break oaths: he is simply drawing attention to God's emphatic promise.)

17. God's promise needs no support: he added an oath for the sake of the *heirs of his promise*, to give them greater assurance of it. The *heirs*, for the writer, are all the men of faith up to his own day (this also will be expanded in chapter 11).

18. The *two acts* are the promise itself, and the oath which confirmed it: they should give *powerful encouragement* to the weakening readers.

us, who have claimed his protection: Christians, the present heirs of his promise (verse 17).

grasping the hope set before us. Another present-future expression for salvation. The *hope* is the heavenly life, already *set before us*, i.e. promised to us, and already to be *grasped* in the present.

19. *an anchor for our lives*. The hope of the future is a means of stability in the uncertainties of their lives, like an anchor holding a ship firm in a storm. The writer has their present crisis in mind, and perhaps also the tragic consequences if they fall away.

It enters in through the veil. A sudden change of metaphor: hope is not simply their assurance for the future, but a present link with heaven. Jesus is already there, as their *forerunner* (verse 20): his presence there is their reason for hoping to enter themselves: so their hope can be said to enter there even now.

where Jesus has entered on our behalf. The theme of *entering the veil* is part of the central imagery of the letter, and derived from the service for the Day of Atonement described in Leviticus 16. This was referred to in 5: 3 and, very allusively, in 2: 17 and 4: 14, and may conveniently be treated fully at this point. It is advisable to become well acquainted with Lev. 16 itself.

It describes an annual ceremony in the Tent, to be performed by Aaron and his successors (Lev. 16: 32), 'to make atonement for the children of Israel because of all their sins once in the year' (Lev. 16: 34). It is thus an annual reconciliation of Israel to God. There are two points in the ceremony which our writer sees as particularly significant: the sacrifice of the bull and goat for the sins of the priesthood and of the whole people (Lev. 16: 11 and 15), and Aaron's entry alone into the holy place with their blood (Lev. 16: 14 and 15). The holy place is where God appears, and the curtain over its entrance is called the veil (Lev. 16: 2): so *entering the veil* means entering the presence of God. Thus, even while in the wilderness, Israel, in the person of the chief priest, entered the presence of God and anticipated the future 'rest'.

Our writer applies this to Christians in this world. Heaven is still in the future: but they have a priest who even now represents them in the presence of God. This is Jesus: and he is in the real 'holy place', heaven itself. (The writer equates Jesus' 'passing through the heavens' (4: 14) with the priest's entering through the veil.) But Christians will one day follow him there: hence he is not only their *high priest* but their *forerunner*: and hence their *hope* can be said to *enter in through the veil* even now.

Notice how our writer's practical purpose is supported by this argument. The Jews had only a mortal high priest annually entering the holy place to God: Christians have Jesus the Son, a priest for ever, who has entered the heavenly presence of God *on our behalf*. So the readers have the strongest possible motive for faithfulness: they are, in this sense, already at their goal.

The writer will elaborate this argument later. Notice that the Day of Atonement imagery is part of his general comparison of Israel in the desert with his readers (see note on 4: 11, page 46). This is why he does not speak of the Temple in Jerusalem, or the annual Day of Atonement of his own time, but of the situation in Leviticus. (Historically the rite probably did not exist in the desert: it grew up after the settlement in Canaan and the founding of the Temple at Jerusalem, and became most prominent after the Exile. It was then 'written back' as part of the original Law at Sinai; so for our writer it originated then.)

20. *having become...Melchizedek*. The writer once again reverts to the point where the argument broke off by echoing its last words (5: 10). But he adds the words *for ever*, which are not in 5: 10, and thus gives a completer quotation of his key text, Ps. 110: 4. His reason is that he is now going to expound that text in full.

Notice how skilfully the writer has brought us back to his main theme. He broke off to warn, and then to encourage: this led to the idea of hope, then to Jesus as the forerunner, and so to Jesus as the high priest. *

MELCHIZEDEK WAS GREATER THAN LEVI

This Melchizedek, king of Salem, priest of God Most 7 High, met Abraham returning from the rout of the kings and blessed him; and Abraham gave him a tithe of 2 everything as his portion. His name, in the first place, means 'king of righteousness'; next he is king of Salem, that is, 'king of peace'. He has no father, no mother, no 3 lineage; his years have no beginning, his life no end. He is like the Son of God: he remains a priest for all time.

Consider now how great he must be for Abraham the 4 patriarch to give him a tithe of the finest of the spoil. The 5 descendants of Levi who take the priestly office are commanded by the Law to tithe the people, that is, their kinsmen, although they too are descendants of Abraham. But Melchizedek, though he does not trace his descent 6

from them, has tithed Abraham himself, and given his
7 blessing to the man who received the promises; and
beyond all dispute the lesser is always blessed by the
8 greater. Again, in the one instance tithes are received by
men who must die; but in the other, by one whom Scrip-
9 ture affirms to be alive. It might even be said that Levi, who
receives tithes, has himself been tithed through Abraham;
10 for he was still in his ancestor's loins when Melchizedek
met him.

* The writer now explores the meaning of Ps. 110: 4 as
applied to Jesus. In this paragraph he considers Melchizedek
himself, and shows that he was a greater priest than the
Levitical priests.

1. The writer picks out from the Gen. 14 story four points
on which to base his argument: Melchizedek's kingship, his
priesthood, his blessing of Abraham, and Abraham's giving
him a tithe of everything.

tithe: a tenth. Used particularly for the tenth of every
Israelite's produce which he gave to the priestly tribe of
Levi, which had no land and therefore produced no crops
(Num. 18: 21–24).

Note that the verb 'to tithe' means to exact or receive
tithes (see verse 5)—not to give them.

2. Melchizedek's kingship. This is described by two
etymological word-plays, on his name and on the name
Salem. This was not mere ingenuity for our writer: in common with most ancient peoples, he thinks of a name as
genuinely descriptive of its owner.

His name...means '*king of righteousness*'. His name can be
taken as a combination of the Hebrew words *melek*, 'king',
and *ṣedeq*, 'righteousness'.

next, he is king of Salem. The writer identifies the place-
name with the Hebrew *shalom*, 'peace'.

Thus Melchizedek is a king of righteousness and of peace.

The appropriateness of this to Jesus is not pointed out: the writer assumes that his readers will see it unaided. Both qualities are commonly attributed to Jesus in the New Testament.

3. Melchizedek's priesthood. The writer wishes to show that Ps. 110: 4 is corroborated, in that Melchizedek is 'a priest for ever' even in Gen. 14. This he does by what most scholars take to be a figurative argument. It depends on the fact that the Old Testament usually names the parents and children, and often notes the birth and death, of its great men. But Melchizedek appears on the scene with no introduction in Gen. 14: 18, and equally suddenly disappears after Gen. 14: 20. He stands therefore as a timeless figure of priesthood, and is in that sense *a priest for all time*—and so 'a priest for ever'.

He is like the Son of God. We might expect the reverse statement, that the Son of God is like Melchizedek. This is a good pointer to the writer's understanding of the way the Old Testament witnesses to the Christian gospel. He uses Old Testament imagery to describe e.g. Jesus' messiahship: but the latter is the great reality, and the former, though the means of understanding the reality, is subordinate, only a foreshadowing. In the perspective of the Christian faith, therefore, the foreshadowing is like its fulfilment—Melchizedek is like Jesus, not *vice versa*.

We can now see why the first two points were picked out of Gen. 14. The writer takes Ps. 110 to refer in its entirety to the Messiah; in verse 1 the Lord enthrones him, in verse 4 declares him a priest for ever. In both the royal and the priestly aspects he is 'in the succession of Melchizedek', because Melchizedek was both king and priest—even, in a sense, a 'priest for ever'.

4–10. The third and fourth points are made together, since both show the same thing: that Melchizedek is greater than Abraham. It is worth outlining the argument first, and then commenting on the details.

The third point is the main subject of these verses; the fourth is mentioned only once, in verses 6*b* and 7, and we will deal with it first. It is that Melchizedek must be greater than Abraham because he blesses him and not *vice versa.*

The third point is about the tithes. The main argument is the same: Melchizedek tithed Abraham, and must therefore be the greater (verse 4). But this brings in the Levites, who also tithe: does this imply that they are as great as Melchizedek? No, because his tithing is greater than theirs, in four ways: (*a*) They tithe only the descendants of Abraham, but Melchizedek tithed Abraham himself (who is necessarily greater than his descendants). (*b*) They do this inferior tithing on the authority of the Law; Melchizedek does his tithing without that authority; but, as it is a superior tithing, he must actually have some even greater authority (verses 5, 6*a*). (*c*) The Levites receive tithes, but are mortal; he receives them, but is alive (verse 8). (*d*) Although Levi now takes tithes, he once paid them to Melchizedek (in the person of his ancestor Abraham) and so confesses his own inferiority.

In this way the writer has used Abraham as a means of demonstrating that Melchizedek was a priest greater than the Levitical priests: and therefore that 'in the succession of Melchizedek' means (among other things) greater than the Jewish priesthood.

5. *although they too* (i.e. their kinsmen) *are descendants of Abraham.* This is obviously meant to add an extra point of contrast between Levites' tithing and Melchizedek's: but its force is not clear. The word *too* in the N.E.B. is not part of the Greek, though it may be implied. If retained, the equality of Levi and the rest of Israel is the point; if omitted, the stress is on the descent of Israel from Abraham. The two following interpretations result.

If the words are meant to emphasize the common descent of Levi and his kinsmen, the point will be: 'In fact even Levi's tithing does not signify his superiority—for we know that those he tithes are as much Abraham's descendants as he is.

Melchizedek's tithing does show his superiority, and so he is a greater priest than Levi.'

If the emphasis is on the descent of Israel from Abraham, the point will be: 'Levi tithes the glorious descendants of Abraham—what a great honour for Levi! But Melchizedek has the even greater honour of tithing Abraham himself!'

6. *though he does not trace his descent from him.* Melchizedek had no Levitical authority, yet he tithed Abraham: he must in fact have had a greater authority still.

given his blessing to the man who received the promises. Abraham's greatness is that he was the first to be promised what our writer interprets as the salvation now realized in Christ. Melchizedek blessed such a man, and so is even greater.

8. *one whom Scripture affirms to be alive.* 'Scripture' means Ps. 110: 4, interpreted as follows. The Son is addressed as a priest for ever in the succession of Melchizedek: so 'for ever' must be part of the meaning of 'in the succession of Melchizedek', and Melchizedek must therefore be alive for ever.

9. *It might even be said*: the writer admits that this last point may be far-fetched. It depends on the idea that Abraham, when Melchizedek met him, could be said to have all his descendants *in his loins*, including his great-grandson Levi. This is not a biological theory, but the common Old Testament idea that a man's descendants are part of him.

The foregoing arguments, and others like them, are not likely to seem strong to us. It is important to see that the writer's main theme is not dependent on them. It depends on his perception that Jesus provides in reality what his Old Testament counterparts only foreshadowed. There are some important arguments to support this, such as the one about sacrifice and obedience in chapter 10. Then there are the smaller arguments about details, as in this chapter, which we may find unconvincing: these are really brought in to support ideas which the writer holds already, on other grounds.

We can now see what the writer understands by *in the*

succession of Melchizedek: righteous and peaceful kingship, combined with a priesthood greater than Levi's and exercised *for ever*. The last two words are the key to the next paragraph. ✳

JESUS IS GREATER THAN LEVI

11 Now if perfection had been attainable through the Levitical priesthood (for it is on this basis that the people were given the Law), what further need would there have been to speak of another priest arising, in the succession of 12 Melchizedek, instead of the succession of Aaron? For a 13 change of priesthood must mean a change of law. And the One here spoken of belongs to a different tribe, no member of which has ever had anything to do with the 14 altar. For it is very evident that our Lord is sprung from Judah, a tribe to which Moses made no reference in speaking of priests.

15 The argument becomes still clearer, if the new priest 16 who arises is one like Melchizedek, owing his priesthood not to a system of earth-bound rules but to the power of a 17 life that cannot be destroyed. For here is the testimony: 'Thou art a priest for ever, in the succession of Melchi-18 zedek.' The earlier rules are cancelled as impotent and 19 useless, since the Law brought nothing to perfection; and a better hope is introduced, through which we draw near to God.

20 How great a difference it makes that an oath was sworn ! 21 There was no oath sworn when those others were made priests; but for this priest an oath was sworn, as Scripture says of him: 'The Lord has sworn and will not go back 22 on his word, "Thou art a priest for ever."' How far

superior must the covenant also be of which Jesus is the 23
guarantor ! Those other priests are appointed in numerous
succession, because they are prevented by death from
continuing in office; but the priesthood which Jesus 24
holds is perpetual, because he remains for ever. That is 25
why he is also able to save absolutely those who approach
God through him; he is always living to plead on their
behalf.

Such a high priest does indeed fit our condition— 26
devout, guileless, undefiled, separated from sinners,
raised high above the heavens. He has no need to offer 27
sacrifices daily, as the high priests do, first for his own
sins and then for those of the people; for this he did once
and for all when he offered up himself. The high priests 28
made by the Law are men in all their frailty; but the
priest appointed by the words of the oath which supersedes the Law is the Son, made perfect now for ever.

✷ The writer has argued Melchizedek's superiority to Levi
on the basis of Gen. 14. He now argues Jesus' superiority to
Levi on the basis of Ps. 110: 4. He appeals to the Psalm (as he
did to Genesis) because he can thus claim Scriptural authority
for his argument. But he appeals also to Jesus' earthly life:
he can mix his authorities in this way because he believes that
the Psalm is really about Jesus.

There are five points in which Jesus is greater than Levi. The
first three are based on the three parts of Ps. 110: 4, 'The
Lord has sworn and will not go back on his word, "Thou
art a priest for ever, in the succession of Melchizedek."' Our
writer works from the last to the first. So verse 4*c*, 'in the
succession of Melchizedek', is quoted in verse 11; 4*b* (and *c*),
'Thou art a priest for ever, in the succession of Melchizedek',
in verse 17; and 4*a* (and *b*), 'The Lord...ever', in verse 21.

The fourth and fifth points are based differently. The method of argument varies from point to point.

11–14. First point, based on Ps. 110: 4c, *in the succession of Melchizedek*. The writer argues from what this text negatively implies. That is, it says Melchizedek, not Aaron—which means, not Levi. Therefore it implies that a priest greater and more effective than the Levites is coming. And history bears this out (verses 13, 14): Jesus was not a Levite, but belonged to Judah.

11. *perfection*: the writer's way of summarizing the whole purpose of religion.

for it is on this basis...given the Law. This certainly means that Law and Levitical priesthood were interdependent, and stand or fall together: verse 12 draws a conclusion from this. It may more precisely mean that the Law depends on the priesthood, in the sense that the priests were necessary to carry out the Law's various instructions.

what further need would there have been to speak? The point depends on chronology: compare the relationship of Gen. 2 and Ps. 95 in 3: 7 — 4: 11. In the writer's view Ps. 110: 4 was spoken during David's reign, when the Levitical system was established and working. To prophesy a non-Levitical priest is an implied criticism of the established Levitical order: it suggests that he will be effective where they are not, and so that he will be greater than they.

the succession of Aaron. Aaron is here regarded as the first of the line of Levitical high priests, so the phrase is equivalent to 'the Levitical priesthood'.

12. A further implication, which the writer points out briefly but does not develop. Since the Law and the Levitical priesthood are interdependent, a non-Levitical priest will bring a new, non-Levitical, Law. This suggests that the existing Law is ineffective. Notice how closely this bears on our writer's purpose, of expounding the obsoleteness of Judaism. It is a point which Paul argues in detail, in Galatians and Romans.

13. *And the One here spoken of*: Jesus. Because he thinks the Psalm is really about Jesus, the writer can bring in a point from Jesus' actual ancestry. He belonged to a tribe quite unconnected with the sacrifices (*the altar*). The prophesied priest, when he came, actually proved to be non-Levitical in descent.

14. *our Lord is sprung from Judah*: adduced as an acknowledged fact. The genealogies in Matt. 1 and Luke 3 trace Jesus' descent from Judah. The Davidic Messiah of the Old Testament prophecies is of Judah, as David was (cf. Micah 5: 2).

to which Moses made no reference in speaking of priests. A reference to Leviticus and Numbers, which contain the instructions about the priests, and which our writer and his contemporaries believed were written by Moses.

15-19. Second point, based on Ps. 110: 4*b*, *Thou art a priest for ever*. The writer sees in these words a reference to Jesus' risen and heavenly life. This is the origin of his priesthood, whereas the origin of the Levites' priesthood is an earthly law.

16. *a system of earthbound rules*: the Law. *Earthbound* is the first hint of the earth–heaven contrast which will occupy chapters 8–10.

the power of a life that cannot be destroyed: a very compressed phrase. It means Jesus' life in heaven, powerful and indestructible because it is the glorious post-resurrection life at God's right hand. Jesus 'owes his priesthood' to it in the sense that God raised him in order to make him high priest. For our writer the resurrection, ascension, entry into heaven, and being seated at the right hand are all parts of God's bestowal of the priesthood upon Jesus.

17. The operative part of the quotation, 4*b*, is added to 4*c* (already quoted in verse 11).

18. The argument here is like that of verse 11 (see notes), but applies to the Law instead of the priesthood. Jesus' heavenly priesthood cancels the basis of the earthly priesthood:

its *earthbound rules*. And his very appointment implies that they were *impotent and useless*: that *the Law* (like the priesthood, verse 11) brought nothing to perfection.

19. *a better hope*, because it really achieves the aim of priesthood—through it *we draw near to God*. The old priesthood did not achieve this.

20–22. Third point, based on the hitherto unquoted Ps. 110: 4*a*, *The Lord has sworn, and will not go back on his word*. The argument is that the Levites, made priests without an oath, must be inferior to Jesus, who was made priest with one. God's irrevocable oath doubles, as it were, the strength of the appointment (cf. 6: 18).

22. One of the writer's additional sentences, adding a further implication of the main argument. Sometimes he does not return to them (e.g. verse 12): sometimes he develops them further on, so that they turn out to have been the first hint of a major theme. The latter is the case here: the contrast of *covenants* underlies the whole letter, and is developed in chapters 8 to 12.

It assumes that *covenant* (like 'law' in verse 12) is interdependent with priesthood: a greater priest brings a greater covenant.

of which Jesus is the guarantor. How he guarantees the new covenant will appear later. There may be the implication that the Levitical priesthood in some sense guaranteed the old covenant: certainly their sacrifices, especially the high priest's on the Day of Atonement, renewed the people's covenant relationship with God.

23–25. Fourth point: a further idea suggested by *priest for ever*. The Levites have to pass on their office to successors when they die; but Jesus, because he lives *for ever*, never has to pass his priesthood to another: he has no equals, no successors.

perpetual: or 'non-transferable'. The point is not its chronological duration, but his permanent possession of it.

25. Another consequence of his living *for ever*: he is always living, as man's representative with God. A contrast with

the Levites could be made here, but the writer is more concerned with the fact itself. Cf. Rom. 8: 34, 'Christ...who is at God's right hand, and indeed pleads our cause', and 1 John 2: 1, 'we have one to plead our cause with the Father, Jesus Christ.'

absolutely: or perhaps temporal in sense, meaning 'always'.

those who approach God through him: Christians, and potentially all men ('many sons', 2: 10).

to plead on their behalf. One aspect of priesthood. Men need someone to approach God for them, because they are prevented by awe and by consciousness of their sins. A priest can approach God in virtue of his office, and so represent those who cannot. This idea is embodied particularly in the Day of Atonement service: our writer sees it perfectly embodied in Christ.

The phrase does not imply that God is unwilling for man to be saved. It implies that he will not tolerate sin: but he has himself sent his Son to overcome this obstacle.

26–28. Fifth point: Jesus is a sinless priest; the Levites are themselves sinners. This is not based on Ps. 110 but on the Christian doctrine previously mentioned in 4: 15 (see note). It may have arisen in the writer's mind out of the implications of verse 25. It is the climax of the paragraph: the new priest has no sin to bar him from the presence of God.

Verses 26, 27 describe his sinlessness; 28 makes a final, complex, and resounding contrast.

26. *high priest.* Since 5: 11 the term *priest* has been used, following the words of Ps. 110. Now the fuller term is resumed, for the rest of the letter.

fit our condition. Cf. 'it was clearly fitting' (2: 10): the needs of man are perfectly met by Christ. In 2: 10 it is man's humanity that requires a human priest: here it is his sin, which requires (on the contrary) a sinless priest.

undefiled: suggested by the elaborate precautions taken by the high priest to prevent defilement.

separated from sinners. Perhaps meaning his sinlessness: but more probably his being in heaven (as the next phrase suggests) and so out of the world where sin and sinners still are.

27. Another mark of Jesus' sinlessness is that he does not have to offer sacrifices for sins, as the Levites do. He did offer a sacrifice, but only once, and then it was a sacrifice of himself. Another apparent aside which turns out to have heralded a main theme.

offer sacrifices daily. Probably a reference to Exod. 29: 38–42, where two lambs are ordered to be sacrificed each day. In contrast, Christ offered one sacrifice.

first for his own sins...people: see 5: 3. This is not the purpose of the daily sacrifices, but of the Day of Atonement ones.

There is thus an apparent contradiction with *daily* in the previous phrase, and several explanations are possible. Perhaps the best is that it is an oversight: the writer inserts the second phrase (which echoes 5: 3 and anticipates 9: 7) without noticing that it does not apply to the daily sacrifices.

for this he did once and for all. The point is in the last four words: it is the contrast between many repeated sacrifices and one unrepeatable. The phrase (one word in Greek) will occur several times more: it sums up so well the finality and completeness of what Jesus did for man in his life and death. *This he did* does not refer in detail to the previous words: it is not being suggested that Christ offered 'for his own sins'.

when he offered up himself. Another implicit contrast, with the offering of animals; to be developed in chapters 9 and 10. The event in the writer's mind is Jesus' death.

28. A fourfold contrast:

Levi	*Jesus*
The high priests	The priest
made by the Law	appointed by the oath
are men	is the Son
in all their frailty	made perfect for ever

men in all their frailty summarizes the weakness of Levi.

the oath which supersedes the Law is God's oath in Ps. 110: 4.
It supersedes it in time, being later than Sinai: and because it
inaugurates the new and better priesthood.

the Son. A contrast not previously made. The emphasis
since chapter 5 has been on the divine appointment of the new
priest. But now chapters 1–4 are brought in: Jesus is not
merely man like the Levites, but the Son become man.

made perfect. In the Greek, the last triumphant word, summarizing Jesus' pre-eminent fitness. God made him 'perfect
through sufferings' (2: 10): Jesus was perfected by his death
(5: 9) and God therefore made him *priest for ever.* ✶

OUR PRIEST IS IN HEAVEN, NOT ON EARTH

Now this is my main point: just such a high priest we **8**
have, and he has taken his seat at the right hand of the
throne of Majesty in the heavens, a ministrant in the real **2**
sanctuary, the tent pitched by the Lord and not by man.
Every high priest is appointed to offer gifts and sacrifices: **3**
hence, this one too must have something to offer. Now **4**
if he had been on earth, he would not even have been a
priest, since there are already priests who offer the gifts
which the Law prescribes, though they minister in a **5**
sanctuary which is only a copy and shadow of the
heavenly. This is implied when Moses, about to erect the
tent, is instructed by God: 'See to it that you make
everything according to the pattern shown you on the
mountain.' But in fact the ministry which has fallen to **6**
Jesus is as far superior to theirs as are the covenant he
mediates and the promises upon which it is legally secured.

✶ This paragraph is a turning-point, like 4: 14–16. It states
the position now reached, and leads on to the next stage of

the argument, the New Covenant which the high priest mediates.

1. *my main point* is the present effective ministry of Jesus. The readers are in present contact with God because their high priest is in heaven. This is their strongest encouragement to be faithful, and not to fall away.

he has taken his seat: cf. 1: 3. The author applies Ps. 110: 1 and 4 to Jesus, who is thus pictured as a seated priest, enthroned at God's right hand. This means that Jesus' intercession is completely effective.

Majesty in the heavens: God (see 1: 3).

2. *a ministrant*: one performing a religious function: here, Jesus representing men, and 'pleading on their behalf' (7: 25). But the point is not what he does, but where he is—in heaven, not in any earthly sanctuary.

the real sanctuary, the tent pitched by the Lord and not by man. A new contrast, between the earthly and heavenly tents. The Tent (cf. 'the veil', 6: 20) described in Exod. 25–27 was the portable place of worship of the Israelites in the desert, pitched wherever they encamped. It contained the holy place where Aaron ministered on the Day of Atonement, and where God was present (Exod. 25: 8, 'let them make me a sanctuary; that I may dwell among them'). It was thus the place where the priest entered God's presence, and the whole people's place of contact with God. Our writer, continuing his comparison with Israel in the desert, says that Christians have a priest in the real dwelling of God, heaven itself, which can therefore be called the *tent pitched by God*.

3. On the principle stated in 5: 1, Jesus as high priest must offer some sacrifice. This verse begins a line of argument (resumed at 9: 6) which is diverted by yet another contrast that occurs to the writer.

4. He has been saying that Jesus is a heavenly, not an earthly, priest: he now heightens the contrast by pointing out that he is an exclusively heavenly priest—he could not possibly have been an earthly priest, since he was not a

Levite. Furthermore, there would be no point in it: earthly priests exist, offering earthly sacrifices; what is needed is a priest in the heavens.

5. *a sanctuary which is only a copy*...A contrast with verse 2, 'the real sanctuary'. The earthly Tent is derived from the real place of God's presence, heaven. This idea is found in Philo, from whom our writer may have learnt it: but, as we should expect, he offers scriptural authority for his statement.

He quotes God's words to Moses in Exod. 25: 40, which probably mean 'follow the instructions I gave you', but he presses the literal meaning of *pattern shown you*, to mean a plan or model shown visually. This means that Moses saw a plan of heaven, or perhaps heaven itself, and modelled the Tent on it. Philo interprets the verse in this way in his *Life of Moses*, ii. 74.

copy and shadow thus express the Platonistic contrast between the heavenly realities and their earthly derivatives: though *shadow* may also have the chronological sense of 'foreshadowing', as it has in 10: 1.

6. The argument suddenly turns to the subject raised in 7: 22, the *covenant* Jesus *mediates*. In that case covenant and priesthood were assumed to go together: here the same is assumed of *covenant* and *ministry*. Later their point of connection is made clear: it is sacrifice, which inaugurates the covenant and is the basis of the ministry.

the promises upon which it is legally secured. A covenant was a legal agreement between parties who promised to keep certain conditions. When the Old Covenant was made, Israel promised to obey the Law (Exod. 24: 7), and God promised that they should be 'a peculiar treasure unto me from among all peoples...a kingdom of priests, and an holy nation' (Exod. 19: 5, 6). *The promises* of the New Covenant are stated by Jeremiah in the words now quoted in 8: 10–12.

Verse 6 thus argues that Jesus' better ministry goes with his better covenant. To this the writer now turns. ✶

THE NEW COVENANT SUCCEEDS WHERE
THE OLD COVENANT FAILED

7 Had that first covenant been faultless, there would have
8 been no need to look for a second in its place. But God,
finding fault with them, says, 'The days are coming, says
the Lord, when I will conclude a new covenant with the
9 house of Israel and the house of Judah. It will not be like
the covenant I made with their forefathers when I took them
by the hand to lead them out of Egypt; because they did
not abide by the terms of that covenant, and I abandoned
10 them, says the Lord. For the covenant I will make with
the house of Israel after those days, says the Lord, is this: I
will set my laws in their understanding and write them
on their hearts; and I will be their God, and they shall be
11 my people. And they shall not teach one another, saying
12 to brother and fellow-citizen, "Know the Lord!" For all
of them shall know me, from small to great; I will be
13 merciful to their wicked deeds, and their sins I will
remember no more at all.' By speaking of a new covenant, he has pronounced the first one old; and anything
that is growing old and ageing will shortly disappear.

✳ So far the writer has spoken of a 'superior covenant' (7: 22,
8: 6), implying that the first covenant is at fault. He now
gives scriptural evidence for this, in the famous passage
Jer. 31: 31–34, about the faults of the Old Covenant and the
need for a new one. The prophecy itself is in the form of a
divine utterance: our writer reiterates this (*God, finding fault
with them, says*), but otherwise he lets it speak for itself.

8. *a new covenant*. Jeremiah prophesied in the late seventh
and early sixth century B.C., when Israel, the northern
kingdom, had already been conquered (in 722 B.C.) and

Judah was about to be (in 587 B.C.). He saw this calamity as a punishment for Israel's breaking of the covenant: God would cease to keep his side of the covenant, and would allow the nation to fall. But this could not be the last word from God, who loved his people: the old covenant was gone, but he would set up a new one.

9. *the covenant I made with their forefathers*: the covenant of Sinai, Exod. 19–24.

they did not abide by the terms. Jeremiah and the other great prophets all accused Israel of breaking their side of the agreement by disobeying God's law.

and I abandoned them. Consequently God did not keep his part, and the covenant was ended. The phrase is in the Septuagint: the Hebrew text reads 'although I was a husband to them'. Another place where the writer's argument depends on his using the LXX.

10–12. The New Covenant has four promises from God (verse 6): (*a*) His laws will be the inner guide of Israel's actions, not a code imposed externally. (*b*) God and Israel will belong to one another. This promise is exactly the same as for the first covenant, but the first covenant lacked effective means of achieving it. (*c*) There will be a universal inner knowledge of God, not dependent on human teaching. (*d*) There will be complete forgiveness for sins: this last is what our writer is most concerned with.

10. *understanding* and *hearts* are synonymous: in Hebrew the heart means the centre of thought, not, as in Western tradition, of the feelings.

13. One comment is added, on the words from verse 8, *new covenant.* To speak of a new one implies that the other is old (cf. the same type of argument in 7: 11): *old* implies *ageing*, and *ageing* leads to disappearing. The point for the readers is: the New Covenant means the end of the Old, which ceases to be a live option. Christianity makes Judaism obsolete. ✳

THE SANCTUARY AND SACRIFICES OF
THE OLD COVENANT

9 The first covenant indeed had its ordinances of divine
2 service and its sanctuary, but a material sanctuary. For a
tent was prepared—the first tent—in which was the
lamp-stand, and the table with the bread of the Presence;
3 this is called the Holy Place. Beyond the second curtain
4 was the tent called the Most Holy Place. Here was a
golden altar of incense, and the ark of the covenant
plated all over with gold, in which were a golden jar
containing the manna, and Aaron's staff which once
5 budded, and the tablets of the covenant; and above it the
cherubim of God's glory, overshadowing the place of
expiation. On these we cannot now enlarge.

6   Under this arrangement, the priests are always entering
7 the first tent in the discharge of their duties; but the
second is entered only once a year, and by the high priest
alone, and even then he must take with him the blood
which he offers on his own behalf and for the people's
8 sins of ignorance. By this the Holy Spirit signifies that
so long as the earlier tent still stands, the way into the
9 sanctuary remains unrevealed. (All this is symbolic,
pointing to the present time.) The offerings and sacrifices
there prescribed cannot give the worshipper inward
10 perfection. It is only a matter of food and drink and
various rites of cleansing—outward ordinances in force
until the time of reformation.

* The two covenants are now compared from the point of
view of their sanctuaries and sacrifices. The relationship of
covenant and sacrifices is still assumed, not explained. Our

writer thinks of the sacrifices as the effective expression (the sacrament) of the covenant: and this, though it is not stated, is clearly the assumption of the Law as represented in Exodus, Leviticus, and Numbers. The priests' continual ministry in the tent is a sign that Israel is God's holy nation, having his presence and keeping his laws.

Verses 1–5 are about the sanctuary, 6–10 about the sacrifices.

1. *ordinances of divine service and its sanctuary.* The *first covenant* was accompanied by the Law, set out in Exod. 20 to Num. 10. Of these 58 chapters, 22 directly concern the tent, priests and divine service: Exod. 26—31, 35—40, Lev. 1—9 and 16.

but a material sanctuary: this prepares for the contrast of 9: 11.

2. *a tent was prepared.* Exod. 26—31 describes the tent, 35—40 its construction. The description is coloured by the form of the subsequent Temple at Jerusalem: the original tent was much simpler.

We have noted previously our writer's complete silence about the Jerusalem Temple of his own time. The immediate reason for this is his 'desert typology', his habit of using Israel's years in the desert as a foreshadowing of the time in which he wrote. We may still wonder how he could be silent about the Temple at any time during the period A.D. 50–90. Two further reasons are here suggested: (*a*) Though a Jew, our writer need not have been a Palestinian Jew: he could have lived all his life in, say, Alexandria, and so have known a Judaism which had no actual contact with the Temple. (*b*) He thinks of the Old and New Covenants as coming one after the other, and of the Old as, for all real purposes, dead. He may therefore deliberately present Judaism to his readers as a thing of the past, to be known from the pages of the Old Testament but not from contemporary life.

If either or both answers are true, it makes little difference to our conclusion about the occasion and date of Hebrews (pp. 5, 9). It is still hard to believe that it could have been written soon after A.D. 70 and have made no reference to the Fall of Jerusalem.

the first tent: not meaning the first in time, but the first to be entered: the main tent, part of which was divided off. Our writer calls them two tents.

the lamp-stand and the table. These stood in the main tent, one each side of the entry to the inner tent (Exod. 26: 35). The *lamp-stand*, with a central stem and three branches each side, became and still is a common Jewish symbol. The table held bread: *bread of the Presence* because it was near the inner tent where God's presence was believed to be. The lamps were always alight and twelve loaves were placed on the table each week: both symbolizing Israel's covenant relation with God (Lev. 24: 1–9).

the Holy Place. The distinction between this and the Most Holy Place is first made in Exod. 26: 33.

3. *the second curtain*. The 'veil' described in Exod. 26: 31. There was a screen at the entrance of the outer tent also (Exod. 26: 36) which the writer thinks of as the first curtain.

Most Holy Place. In Hebrew literally 'the Holy of Holies'.

4. *Here was a golden altar of incense*. Exod. 30: 6 says it stands 'before the veil...before the mercy seat', and Exod. 40: 26 shows that this means outside the veil. Our writer seems to have followed Exod. 30: 6 and to have thought that the golden altar was inside the veil.

4, 5. *the ark of the covenant*. This was a gold-plated chest, carried on poles when Israel was on the march. It was the symbol of the covenant both by its contents and by its cover. (*a*) Its contents: the *jar of manna* and *Aaron's staff* were both placed before the ark (Exod. 16: 34, Num. 17: 10), not inside it; our writer probably conjectures that they were placed inside. Both recalled God's aid to the wandering Israelites, and the rod was a sign of Aaron's election to the priesthood. The *tablets of the covenant* were the two stone tablets engraved with the terms of Israel's obligations under the covenant. They were put inside the ark (Deut. 10: 5) and this gave it its name *ark of the covenant* (Num. 10: 33). (*b*) Its cover (verse 5): the top of the ark had a different purpose: it was thought of as the place where God came (Lev. 16: 2, 13) as if to his throne, with the two figures of the cherubim like royal attendants each side.

5. *the cherubim* are winged figures at each end of the ark (Exod. 25: 18–20). Cherubim were God's angelic attendants: they appear in the heavenly vision of Ezek. 10.

of God's glory: literally 'of the glory', i.e. the *shekinah*, the pillar of cloud and fire that marked God's presence. It led Israel through the desert (Exod. 13: 21), and covered the tent when it had been erected (Exod. 40: 34). In Lev. 16: 2, Aaron is warned that God will 'appear in the cloud upon the mercy-seat': the cherubim thus attend upon 'the glory'.

overshadowing the place of expiation. A reference to Exod. 25: 20. The *place of expiation* (R.V. 'mercy-seat') was the golden lid covering the ark. On the Day of Atonement it was sprinkled with the blood of the bull and goat (Lev. 16: 14, 15), and thus Israel was reunited to God by means of the sacrificial blood.

6, 7. The outer tent is accessible, but entry to the Most Holy Place is severely limited: only the high priest may enter, *only once a year*, and *even then* only by virtue of the blood of the two animals just killed. Even he needs sacrifice before he can enter.

the blood which he offers. On the Day of Atonement the blood is sprinkled upon and before the mercy-seat (Lev. 16: 14 f.) and in that sense is offered to God.

8. *the Holy Spirit signifies*: because the arrangements are all laid down in the scriptures which the Spirit inspired.

so long as the earlier tent still stands, i.e. during the era of the Old Covenant. The writer is not thinking historically, for the tent had not stood since the desert wanderings had ceased.

the way into the sanctuary remains unrevealed; i.e. there is no open access to God's presence.

9*a*. (*All this is symbolic...*). The imperfections of the Old Covenant foreshadow the perfections of the New.

9*b*, 10. The writer generalizes about the sacrifices of the Old Covenant, and makes a new contrast—they are outward acts, but men need *inward perfection* (as Jeremiah's prophecy indicates, 8: 10). This is the basic failure of the old covenant and its sacrifices: they are on the wrong level. Man needs *inward perfection*, and a new covenant and sacrifice that will give him it. To this the writer now turns. ✳

THE SANCTUARY AND SACRIFICE OF CHRIST

11 But now Christ has come, high priest of good things already in being. The tent of his priesthood is a greater and more perfect one, not made by men's hands, that is, not
12 belonging to this created world; the blood of his sacrifice is his own blood, not the blood of goats and calves; and thus he has entered the sanctuary once and for all and
13 secured an eternal deliverance. For if the blood of goats and bulls and the sprinkled ashes of a heifer have power to hallow those who have been defiled and restore their
14 external purity, how much greater is the power of the blood of Christ; he offered himself without blemish to God, a spiritual and eternal sacrifice; and his blood will cleanse our conscience from the deadness of our former ways and fit us for the service of the living God.

✳ This paragraph lists the perfections of Christ's sacrifice corresponding to the imperfections just described. It also recapitulates points from 7: 26–28.

11*a*. Christ's priesthood brings *good things already in being* or (N.E.B. footnote) *which were* (or *are*) *to be*. The old priesthood only pointed to them (verse 9*a*). The *good things* are all the benefits of the new covenant—access to God, perfection, the sabbath rest. The uncertainty whether the tense is present or future does not affect the point. The good things *were to be* before Christ came, and are *in being* or *to be*, depending on whether they are thought of as possessed now or in heaven.

11 *b*. Christ's priesthood is exercised in heaven (contrast with verse 1). A repetition of the point in 8: 1–5.

12 *a*. His sacrifice is in his own blood (contrast with verse 7*b*).

12 *b*. (i) He entered heaven by virtue of his own blood, i.e. his self-sacrifice gained him access (contrast verse 7*b*). (ii) He entered once and remains there, not entering and leaving every year, i.e. he is always with God (contrast verse 7*a*).

13, 14. His inward sacrifice will give inward purity (contrast verses 9*b*, 10). It is accepted that the external sacrifices gave external cleansing (verse 13): it must follow that Christ's *spiritual and eternal sacrifice* can give us cleansing of *conscience* and make us *fit for the service of the living God.*

13. *the sprinkled ashes of a heifer.* In Num. 19: 1–10 directions are given for using these as a means of cleansing after certain types of ritual impurity.

14. *he offered himself without blemish to God*: cf. 7: 27. This is the inner reality of Christ's sacrifice, and the meaning of *the blood of Christ.* As in Paul, *blood* refers both to sacrifice and to Jesus' death, and so can signify the whole self-offering of Jesus which was brought to its climax by his death. This inward meaning is finally expounded in chapter 10. ✻

CHRIST'S SACRIFICE INAUGURATES
THE NEW COVENANT

And therefore he is the mediator of a new covenant, or 15 testament, under which, now that there has been a death to bring deliverance from sins committed under the former covenant, those whom God has called may receive

16 the promise of the eternal inheritance. For where there is a testament it is necessary for the death of the testator to be

17 established. A testament is operative only after a death: it

18 cannot possibly have force while the testator is alive. Thus we find that the former covenant itself was not inaugu-

19 rated without blood. For when, as the Law directed, Moses had recited all the commandments to the people, he took the blood of the calves, with water, scarlet wool, and marjoram, and sprinkled the law-book itself and all

20 the people, saying, 'This is the blood of the covenant

21 which God has enjoined upon you.' In the same way he also sprinkled the tent and all the vessels of divine ser-

22 vice with blood. Indeed, according to the Law, it might almost be said, everything is cleansed by blood and without the shedding of blood there is no forgiveness.

23 If, then, these sacrifices cleanse the copies of heavenly things, those heavenly things themselves require better

24 sacrifices to cleanse them. For Christ has entered, not that sanctuary made by men's hands which is only a symbol of the reality, but heaven itself, to appear now before

25 God on our behalf. Nor is he there to offer himself again and again, as the high priest enters the sanctuary year by

26 year with blood not his own. If that were so, he would have had to suffer many times since the world was made. But as it is, he has appeared once and for all at the climax of history to abolish sin by the sacrifice of himself.

27 And as it is the lot of men to die once, and after death

28 comes judgement, so Christ was offered once to bear the burden of men's sins, and will appear a second time, sin done away, to bring salvation to those who are watching for him.

✻ Verse 15 states that Christ's death has brought about the *new covenant*: verses 16–18 explain how. The explanation rests on the two senses of the Greek word *diatheke*—the religious sense of an agreement between God and man (see note on 8: 6, p. 79), and the sense of a person's 'will', by which he arranges for the disposal of his possessions after his death. The latter meaning occupies verses 16 and 17, and the former (which is the more important for our writer) verses 18–28.

15. The Greek word *diatheke* suggests two connections with death: (*a*) a *death to bring deliverance from sins*, a sin-offering, precedes a 'covenant' between God and man. (*b*) Death always precedes an inheritance made by a will (a 'last will and testament' in the English phrase): the *eternal inheritance* of Christians follows upon Jesus' death. As elsewhere, our writer now enlarges upon the two ideas, in reverse order.

covenant, or testament, in the N.E.B. is an explanatory double translation to prepare us for the two senses. In the Greek there is the one word only.

16, 17. The benefits of a will cannot be received until the testator is dead: they follow his death and require it. Christ's benefits, then, similarly follow and require his death. It is not a satisfactory analogy, because the underlying reasons are quite different in each case. The writer seems to sense this, and turns to the other sense of *diatheke*.

18. As he reverts to the idea of death preceding a covenant, he shifts its emphasis. He is about to quote the story of the covenant sacrifice in Exodus 24: 3–8, but this is not a sin-offering: its climax is the blood-sprinkling on the altar and the people. So he shifts the emphasis from death as such to *blood*, thus resuming the theme of Christ's blood in verses 12–14.

19–22. These verses are remarkable for the line of their argument and the inaccuracy of their Old Testament references. The argument is the main thing, and we will outline it before noting the inaccuracies.

(a) *Argument*. First (19, 20) comes the reference to Exod. 24: 3–8, emphasizing its climax, the blood-sprinkling (which our writer probably understands as a cleansing ceremony). Then (verse 21) comes a reference to the next recorded occasion of blood-sprinkling: the consecration of the tent and the priests (Lev. 8), when the blood signifies cleansing. (This latter event might reasonably be counted part of the inauguration of the covenant too.) From these two stories the writer ventures a general principle, that cleansing and forgiveness require *the shedding* (or perhaps *the sprinkling*) *of blood*.

Note the effect of verse 21: it shifts the emphasis away from the covenant idea and back to that of the priestly ministry in the tent. The covenant-sacrifice idea returns later.

(b) *Inaccuracies*. First, *water, scarlet wool, and marjoram* are not mentioned in Exod. 24. They are part of certain cleansing rites (Lev. 14: Num. 19: 6) quite unconnected with the in-auguration of the covenant, though of course they are part of the covenant's provisions. Next, Moses sprinkled the altar (Exod. 24: 6), not the book, though he read from the book (Exod. 24: 7). Next, he anointed (verse 21), not *sprinkled*, the tent and its contents (Lev. 8: 10). What he *sprinkled* was the altar (Lev. 8: 15, 19), and the priests (Lev. 8: 30).

The writer's mistakes, due probably to his quoting from memory, do not, however, cause him seriously to violate the meaning of these details. They do all signify cleansing, or something like it: he attaches them with some appropriateness to the inauguration of the covenant and the tent. Given his methods, then, he may be said to have made his point success-fully in verse 22—a point which he introduces modestly with the words *it might almost be said* as a suggestion rather than an assertion.

23, 24. This principle about *blood* is now applied to Jesus' sacrifice. The first words, *these sacrifices cleanse the copies of heavenly things*, refer to verse 21. There the writer alluded to Lev. 8, the account of the consecration of the tent, its contents, and Aaron and the other priests. All these things—i.e. the whole system centred in the tent—he now calls *the copies of heavenly things*, because they are the earthly copies of the new system centred in heaven. The tent system was inaugurated by sacrifices (whose blood was sprinkled on it, verse 21): the heavenly system (*the heavenly things*) must have been inaugurated by *better sacrifices*, because (verse 24) it is the heavenly reality with the real priest in God's real presence.

23. *these sacrifices*: the deaths involved in the shedding of blood (verse 22).

cleanse. The verb picks up *cleansed by blood* from the previous verse.

better sacrifices: the plural is caused by the parallelism of the verse, and is not significant. Later it is clear that there is only one better sacrifice.

to cleanse them. This also is a result of the parallelism: the writer is not suggesting that heaven needs cleansing. *Cleanse* is appropriate to the earthly tent, though it does not occur in verse 21, where the main idea is really inauguration.

The second half of verse 23 could be paraphrased: 'the heavenly ministry requires a better sacrifice to inaugurate it'.

24. *heaven itself.* The writer drops the 'heavenly sanctuary' language, so as to name only the reality itself. He does not think that heaven really has any visible similarity to the tent.

to appear now before God on our behalf: the reality foreshadowed by the high priest's entry 'through the veil'. Cf. 'plead on their behalf', 7: 25 (and note), and 'ministry', 8: 6.

25. A look back, to the sacrifice which made Christ's priesthood possible. It is not repeated annually, like the earthly high priest's.

26. A new variant of the contrast of 'once' and 'again and again'. The high priest's annual entry involves annual sacrifices, so if Christ were offering himself repeatedly, he would have to die repeatedly: but he *appeared once and for all*, as the gospel tells us. His offering is over, so he has entered heaven and remains there as our representative.

to abolish sin by the sacrifice of himself, cf. 7: 27, 9: 14. To be developed in chapter 10: but first the writer's thought is carried forward, to the ultimate purpose of Christ's work.

27, 28. The idea of death leads to that of judgement, which Jews and Christians expected at the end of the present age. Christ, like all men, dies only once: but his death is a sacrifice for men's sins, and so results not in judgement but in salvation.

28. *to bear the burden of* (or, N.E.B. footnote, *to remove*) *men's sins*: quoted from Isa. 53: 12, where the Servant of the Lord is said to do this by his death. Commonly applied in the New Testament to Jesus, perhaps in his own teaching (Mark 10: 45, 'a ransom for many').

a second time: the only explicit statement in the New Testament that Christ's Parousia will be a *second* appearing. Our writer may also be thinking of the Day of Atonement, when the high priest came out of the tent (Lev. 16: 24), having done away sin for the people.

sin done away: literally 'without sin', i.e. not concerned with sin (as he was when he *appeared once and for all*, the first time), but with salvation.

those who are watching for him. Cf. Jesus' command to 'keep awake' for the return of 'the master of the house' (Mark 13: 35), and Paul in 1 Thess. 1: 10, 'to wait expectantly for the appearance from heaven of his Son Jesus'. Many in the early church thought of themselves as a fellowship waiting for the speedy return of Christ. Similarly our writer may think of them as the Israelites awaiting the high priest's reappearance from the tent. *

THE PERFECTION OF CHRIST'S SACRIFICE

10 For the Law contains but a shadow, and no true image, of the good things which were to come; it provides for the same sacrifices year after year, and with these it can

never bring the worshippers to perfection for all time.
If it could, these sacrifices would surely have ceased to be 2
offered, because the worshippers, cleansed once for all,
would no longer have any sense of sin. But instead, in 3
these sacrifices year after year sins are brought to mind,
because sins can never be removed by the blood of bulls 4
and goats.

That is why, at his coming into the world, he says: 5

'Sacrifice and offering thou didst not desire,
But thou hast prepared a body for me.
Whole-offerings and sin-offerings thou didst not delight 6
in.
Then I said, "Here am I: as it is written of me in the 7
scroll,
I have come, O God, to do thy will."'

First he says, 'Sacrifices and offerings, whole-offerings and 8
sin-offerings, thou didst not desire nor delight in'—
although the Law prescribes them—and then he says, 'I 9
have come to do thy will.' He thus annuls the former to
establish the latter. And it is by the will of God that we 10
have been consecrated, through the offering of the body
of Jesus Christ once and for all.

* The writer now caps his argument by giving his deepest
reason for the superiority of Christ's sacrifice—its quality of
complete obedience to God.

1–4. A fresh point about the repetition of the old sacrifices.
The Law shows that it does not even expect to give *perfection*,
by the very fact that it commands repeated sacrifices: if they
were going to give perfection they would not need repetition.
They fail to give it because they are only animal sacrifices: the
Law has no means of effectively removing sin.

1. *image* signifies near-identity, practically 'reality'.

good things which were to come: the Christian salvation (cf. 9: 11).

perfection for all time: see note on 7: 11.

2. If the sacrifices had worked, the worshippers would not need to repeat them. Their repetition demonstrates their ineffectiveness.

3. And worse, the repetition actually provides a reminder that sin is still there.

4. The fundamental reason: animal sacrifice and sin are on different levels. In 9: 9, 10 the difference was expressed by the contrast 'inward perfection: outward ordinances'. But God has now provided an appropriate remedy (verses 5–10).

5. *That is why*: i.e. because of the fundamental ineffectiveness.

at his coming into the world, he says. The writer's application of the following quotation: he makes it the Son's words when he became man.

5–7. Quotation: Ps. 40: 6–8, the Psalmist speaking to God, saying that man's obedience is what God requires, and not sacrifices. Application: the Son speaking to God. The words *I have come* (verse 7) enable the writer to refer it to *his coming into the world*.

The Psalm fits the writer's purpose perfectly, because it sees that obedience is the real remedy for sin. Our writer adds nothing to this principle: what he adds is (*a*) that Jesus has actually achieved this obedience, and (*b*) that this quality of obedience is what makes his death an acceptable offering to God.

5. *thou hast prepared a body for me*: the LXX text. The Hebrew says 'thou hast given me an open ear'—i.e. 'thou hast given me obedience'. The writer uses the LXX, and can thus see in *a body* a reference to Christ's death.

7. Obedience is the subject of the last line of the Psalm: this enables our writer to apply the entire quotation to Christ's obedience and death.

as it is written of me in the scroll. In the Psalm, this may refer to the copy of the Law made for the Israelite king (Deut. 17: 18) and given to him at his coronation ('gave him the testimony', 2 Kings 11: 12) so that he might know and obey God's will. In applying it to Christ, our writer probably takes *scroll* to mean the Old Testament, with its Messianic prophecies.

8–10. The quotation is now expounded to signify Christ's obedience and death, and the ending of the old sacrifices.

8. Lines 1 and 3 of the quotation are combined, to make a single comprehensive rejection of the sacrificial system.

although the Law prescribes them. The writer does not mean that the Law was not given by God, but that its ordinances did not represent his full will.

9. *I have come to do thy will.* The words express obedience to God: so they can here stand for Christ's obedience (5: 8).

He annuls the former to establish the latter. The effect of the psalm verses quoted is to replace sacrifice with obedience.

10. Lines 2 (*a body*) and 5 (*to do thy will*) of the quotation are combined, to signify obedience in death.

by the will of God: literally 'by this will'—God's will obeyed by Christ, or, Christ's obedience to God's will.

we have been consecrated. The achievement of the purpose described in 2: 11, 'a consecrating priest and those whom he consecrates': Christians are made fit to approach God.

offering of the body of Jesus Christ: Christ's death, his supreme act of obedience. The sacrificial language of verse 10 reflects the Day of Atonement: the death of the bull and goat enabled the priest to enter the tent, and Jesus' obedience in death enabled him to enter heaven. This consecrates us, in that it enables us to come to God.

The heart of Christ's offering is thus his obedience: the proper human attitude to God, as the Psalmist saw. It is an adequate remedy for sin because it is on the same level— human, inward, the right relationship to God. The writer does not say, but doubtless holds, that sin is fundamentally disobedience to God (as in the story of Gen. 3); obedience is therefore its proper remedy, the perfect 'sacrifice for sins' (verse 12). ✳

THE FINALITY OF CHRIST'S SACRIFICE FOR SIN

11 Every priest stands performing his service daily and offering time after time the same sacrifices, which can 12 never remove sins. But Christ offered for all time one sacrifice for sins, and took his seat at the right hand of God, 13 where he waits henceforth until his enemies are made his 14 footstool. For by one offering he has perfected for all 15 time those who are thus consecrated. Here we have also 16 the testimony of the Holy Spirit: he first says, 'This is the covenant which I will make with them after those days, says the Lord: I will set my laws in their hearts and write 17 them on their understanding'; then he adds, 'and their sins 18 and wicked deeds I will remember no more at all.' And where these have been forgiven, there is no longer any offering for sin.

✳ The perfection of Christ's obedience in death makes further sacrifices for sins unnecessary: it is final, *for all time.*

11–13. A last detailed contrast of the old sacrifices with the new:

Old	New
Every priest	But Christ
stands	took his seat
performing his sacrifice	where he waits
offering	offered
time after time	for all time
the same sacrifices	one sacrifice for sins

12. *took his seat*, his offering finished.

13. The second part of Ps. 110: 1, quoted only once previously, in 1: 13. The idea of Christ's reigning in heaven till the final conquest of evil is not developed by our writer. Although in speaking of Christ's state in heaven he emphatically uses the image of being seated, in speaking of Christ's activity in heaven he uses chiefly the language of ministry (8: 6) and pleading (7: 25). The combination arises from the use of Ps. 110: 1 *and* 4: the image is of a reigning priest, and the idea is that Christ's perfect representation of man is perfectly accepted by God and so completely effective.

14. *he has perfected*: this sounds as if Christians are actually perfect, which the writer clearly does not believe. The idea is that they are *consecrated*, and on the way to actual perfection: but since this depends on the finished offering of Christ, it can be regarded as in principle achieved already. 'He has done finally the act which bestows perfection.'

15–18. Scriptural support for the finality, by an ingenious use of Jer. 31: 31–4, quoted earlier. The argument is as follows: (i) *he first says*: in Jer. 31: 33 *the Holy Spirit* says that under the new covenant man will obey God from his heart (verse 16); (ii) *then he adds*: in Jer. 31: 34 he says that God will no longer remember man's sins (verse 17); (iii) this must mean that God will have forgiven them (verse 18 *a*); (iv) in which case sin-offerings will have no need to exist, and will exist *no longer* (verse 18 *b*).

The rather tortuous form of this argument does not invalidate its meaning, however: 'in an era of sinlessness, sin-offerings will not exist' is cogent enough. If Jesus has in principle brought in an era of sinlessness, men need not make sin-offerings.

This repetition of the previous quotation gives a sense of unity to the section on the New Covenant, 8: 7 — 10: 18. *

97

DRAW NEAR WITH FAITH

19 So now, my friends, the blood of Jesus makes us free to
20 enter boldly into the sanctuary by the new, living way
which he has opened for us through the curtain, the way
21 of his flesh. We have, moreover, a great priest set over
22 the household of God; so let us make our approach in
sincerity of heart and full assurance of faith, our guilty
hearts sprinkled clean, our bodies washed with pure water.
23 Let us be firm and unswerving in the confession of our
24 hope, for the Giver of the promise may be trusted. We
ought to see how each of us may best arouse others to
25 love and active goodness, not staying away from our
meetings, as some do, but rather encouraging one another,
all the more because you see the Day drawing near.

✻ This passage should be closely compared with 4: 14–16.
Its content is very similar (4: 14 and 10: 21f. especially). It
states the present benefits of Christ's high priesthood, and
urges the readers to respond by faith. Its function in the
letter is also the same: it sums up the previous chapters and
begins the next main section. The last third of the letter really
begins here, not at 11: 1.

Verses 19–21 state that we have access to God through
Jesus; verses 22–25 urge us to respond, in worship (22), faith
(23), and fellowship (24, 25).

19. *the blood of Jesus makes us free to enter.* The consequence
of the sacrifice on the Day of Atonement was that the high
priest could enter with the blood. In 9: 12 it was said that
Christ entered by virtue of his own blood: here, that Christians
may do so. Their relationship to Christ is thus very
close indeed, because of his self-identification with man. In
Jewish thought a representative was practically identical
with those he represented.

into the sanctuary: heaven itself (9: 24). Cf. Eph. 2: 6, 'in Christ Jesus he raised us up and enthroned us with him in the heavenly realms'. Our writer's emphasis on the future does not rule out a strong doctrine of present access to God, and present unity with Christ.

20. *the new, living way*: living because he is alive in heaven, and we enter by our union with the one who represents us.

through the curtain: 'through the veil' (6: 20).

the way of his flesh, or (N.E.B. footnote) *through the curtain of his flesh*. In the Greek it is not clear whether *of his flesh* applies to *way* or *curtain*. The first version means that we enter by means *of his flesh*, i.e. his human self offered in death. The second means this, but adds a further metaphor—his *flesh* was the very curtain that he opened. This means that the destruction of his body in death was the way or means by which he entered. Cf. the dramatic incident of Mark 15: 38, when at Jesus' death 'the curtain of the temple was torn in two', which in some form must be known to our writer.

21. *a great priest set over the household of God*. A reference to 3: 6, which has the effect of recalling the earlier chapters and drawing the first two thirds of the letter together. Cf. 'the Son' in 7: 28.

22. *let us make our approach*. The way is open, but the worshippers have the responsibility of using it. A similar sequence of thought is very characteristic of Paul—e.g. Col. 3: 1, 'Were you not raised to life in Christ? Then aspire to the realm above, where Christ is.'

our guilty hearts sprinkled clean, our bodies washed with pure water. The parallelism of the phrases shows that they must be taken together. The first phrase echoes 9: 14, and 9: 19, the covenant inauguration; the second refers to baptism. Christians enter the New Covenant by a rite analogous to the blood-sprinkling of Exod. 24: 8.

Christ's blood is not mentioned here, partly to avoid a clash of imagery (blood/water), but also because the writer consistently avoids any suggestion that Christ's blood is materially carried or sprinkled (cf. 9: 12, 14).

Verse 22 as a whole expresses the Christian response to salvation in terms of worship: cf. Romans 12: 1, where Paul, having completed his main argument, says, 'Therefore, my brothers, I implore you...to offer your very selves to him: a living sacrifice, dedicated and fit for his acceptance, the worship offered by mind and heart.'

23. *Let us be firm and unswerving.* The special purpose of the letter reappears. This is the beginning of the 'Call to Faith' of the last three chapters.

the confession of our hope means the avowal (perhaps public avowal) of Christianity.

the Giver of the promise may be trusted. The 'faithfulness' or trustworthiness of God elicits faith: his *promise* is the ground of *our hope*.

24, 25. The response of Christian fellowship. Apart from 6: 10, the mutual relationship of the readers has not been mentioned so far. Here we have evidence of dissension among them: some are *staying away from our meetings*, and it is implied that there is a lack of *love and active goodness*. In chapter 13 a good deal is said about mutual love.

all the more because you see the Day drawing near. The 'Day of the Lord' of Old Testament prophecy. For Christians it was a source of hope, so that its nearness is a further incentive to faith. The remaining chapters are dominated by the idea of the future hope, just as the previous ones have been by the idea of present access. ✳

A FOURTH WARNING:

DESERTERS BRING JUDGEMENT ON THEMSELVES

26 For if we persist in sin after receiving the knowledge of
27 the truth, no sacrifice for sins remains: only a terrifying expectation of judgement and a fierce fire which will

consume God's enemies. If a man disregards the Law of 28
Moses, he is put to death without pity on the evidence of
two or three witnesses. Think how much more severe 29
a penalty that man will deserve who has trampled under
foot the Son of God, profaned the blood of the covenant
by which he was consecrated, and affronted God's
gracious Spirit! For we know who it is that has said, 30
'Justice is mine: I will repay'; and again, 'The Lord will
judge his people.' It is a terrible thing to fall into the 31
hands of the living God.

✻ This warning has the same form as the previous two:

(a) the principle	3: 14		6: 4-6	10: 26, 27
(b) its elaboration	3: 15 — 4: 11		6: 7, 8a	10: 28-30
(c) a brief and terrible warning	4: 12, 13		6: 8b	10: 31

26, 27. The warning is in terms of sacrifice. If a Christian
persists in sin he is repudiating Christ's sacrifice, and bringing
judgement upon himself.

26. *no sacrifice for sins remains*: i.e. for the sinner. There is
only Christ's, and the sinner is refusing it by his persistent
sin.

a fierce fire. Cf. 6: 8, 'the end of that is burning', and 12: 29.

28, 29. An expansion of the argument in the first warning
(2: 2, 3). The better covenant brings the heavier penalties.

28. Deut. 17: 2-6 is the reference: the sin in question
there is 'transgressing the covenant' and worshipping 'other
gods'—apostasy.

29. *how much more severe a penalty*: the one described in
verse 27, judgement and annihilation. The enormity of the
sin is brought out by three strong clauses: (a) *trampled under
foot the Son of God*—shown deliberate and brutal contempt
for Christ; (b) *profaned the blood of the covenant* (cf. 9: 20

and 10: 22): treated the holy as if it were not holy, and so in effect repudiated it; (c) *affronted God's gracious Spirit*. Cf. Mark 3: 29, where Jesus says 'whoever slanders the Holy Spirit can never be forgiven; he is guilty of eternal sin'. The Spirit is God working in a man: to persist in sin is to repudiate his guidance.

30. Quotations: Deut. 32: 35, 36, God's declaration of his judgement on sinful Israel.

31. *fall into the hands*. Probably an allusion to Ecclesiasticus 2: 18, 'We will fall into the hands of the Lord', where the reference is to the Lord's mercy: our writer turns the words to the opposite purpose.

the living God: a common Old Testament expression, connoting God's real and active power. ✻

REMEMBER YOUR PAST ENDURANCE

32 Remember the days gone by, when, newly enlightened, you met the challenge of great sufferings and held firm.
33 Some of you were abused and tormented to make a public show, while others stood loyally by those who were
34 so treated. For indeed you shared the sufferings of the prisoners, and you cheerfully accepted the seizure of your possessions, knowing that you possessed something
35 better and more lasting. Do not then throw away your
36 confidence, for it carries a great reward. You need endurance, if you are to do God's will and win what he has
37 promised. For 'soon, very soon' (in the words of Scripture), 'he who is to come will come; he will not
38 delay; and by faith my righteous servant shall find life;
39 but if a man shrinks back, I take no pleasure in him.' But we are not among those who shrink back and are lost; we have the faith to make life our own.

✲ 32–9. As before, the writer turns from dire warning to encouragement. He reminds his readers of a past occasion when they *held firm* in *great sufferings* (verse 32), the same occasion previously described in 6: 10 as 'when you rendered service to his people'. Verses 33 and 34 refer to some sort of persecution involving imprisonment and seizure of possessions. Apparently some had been *abused and tormented*, by being imprisoned: others stood by them and shared their sufferings. *The seizure of your possessions* seems to imply that all of them had suffered in this particular way.

It is not possible to identify this incident: the imprisonment could have been by local authorities, but the seizure of possessions could have been official confiscation, public looting, or both. Nothing necessarily indicates an official persecution, and we read in 12: 4 that no one had yet suffered to the point of bloodshed. The sort of riots narrated in Acts, following upon missionary work (e.g. Acts 17: 5, at Thessalonica), could have occurred anywhere, and this is probably such an incident. It is sometimes suggested that it could have occurred during the Jewish troubles in Rome, caused by (probably) the presence of Christians there, which led to the Jews being expelled from the city in A.D. 49. This would agree with the other indications that the letter was written to Rome (see p. 6), but it is no more than a possibility.

32. *newly enlightened*, recently baptized (cf. 6: 4).

33. *a public show*, not (as it literally means) in the arena, but perhaps as a public deterrent.

34. *shared the sufferings*: suffered in some way, by their association with them; physically, or by sympathy.

knowing that you possessed something better and more lasting. Their future salvation: the *great reward* of the next verse, the 'city which is to come' of 13: 14.

35. *your confidence*. The confidence they exhibited previously. The Greek word is *parresia*: it occurs in 3: 6 (translated as 'fearless' in the N.E.B.). The other two occurrences, in 4: 16 and 10: 19 (translated as 'boldly', N.E.B.), show

that it is not self-confidence, but rests upon Jesus' presence on their behalf in heaven.

36. *endurance*. The Greek noun and its verb are prominent in this paragraph and the first paragraph of chapter 12. In verse 32 the verb lies behind the translation 'met...and held firm'. The readers need the same quality now.

if you are to do God's will echoes 'I have come, O God, to do thy will' (10: 7). Christians are to follow Christ's obedience.

37, 38. 'soon, very soon' is from Isa. 10: 25 and 26: 20, which both refer to the nearness of God's judgement. What follows is a very free quotation from Habakkuk 2: 3, 4.

37. *he who is to come*. In Hab. 2, the Messiah: for our writer, Jesus.

38. *my righteous servant...a man...* In Hab. 2, the Messiah: but for our writer, the faithful Christian and the backslider respectively.

39. Verse 38 is now applied to the readers, with their alternatives of faithfulness or backsliding. The writer states that they are among the faithful, as if it were a certain fact: it is his way of encouraging them to make it a fact.

Paul appeals to the same text in Habakkuk, as a basis for his argument about faith in Galatians and Romans. He means something rather different from our writer: faith, for Paul, is the opposite of 'keeping the law' (Rom. 3: 28): it is trust in God as opposed to trust in one's own goodness. What our writer means by 'faith' he now explains in the next verse.

'*The Shadow and the Real*'. The argument of chapters 5 — 10 may now be stated in terms of their N.E.B. heading. The Old Covenant, with its high priests repeatedly offering animal sacrifices and entering the earthly tent to remove sins and appear before God for the people, was a shadow. It looked forward to the reality, the New Covenant established by Jesus, the real representative of man, whose obedience to God was the real remedy for sin, and who is really with God in heaven to represent us. ✳

A Call to Faith

FAITH: ABEL TO ABRAHAM

AND WHAT IS FAITH? Faith gives substance to our **11**
hopes, and makes us certain of realities we do not
see.

It is for their faith that the men of old stand on record. 2

By faith we perceive that the universe was fashioned by 3
the word of God, so that the visible came forth from the
invisible.

By faith Abel offered a sacrifice greater than Cain's, 4
and through faith his goodness was attested, for his
offerings had God's approval; and through faith he
continued to speak after his death.

By faith Enoch was carried away to another life with- 5
out passing through death; he was not to be found, because God has taken him. For it is the testimony of
Scripture that before he was taken he had pleased God,
and without faith it is impossible to please him; for 6
anyone who comes to God must believe that he exists and
that he rewards those who search for him.

By faith Noah, divinely warned about the unseen 7
future, took good heed and built an ark to save his
household. Through his faith he put the whole world in
the wrong, and made good his own claim to the righteousness which comes of faith.

By faith Abraham obeyed the call to go out to a land 8
destined for himself and his heirs, and left home without
knowing where he was to go. By faith he settled as an 9

alien in the land promised him, living in tents, as did
10 Isaac and Jacob, who were heirs to the same promise. For
he was looking forward to the city with firm foundations,
whose architect and builder is God.

11 By faith even Sarah herself received strength to con-
ceive, though she was past the age, because she judged
12 that he who had promised would keep faith; and therefore from one man, and one as good as dead, there
sprang descendants numerous as the stars or as the
countless grains of sand on the sea-shore.

13 All these persons died in faith. They were not yet in
possession of the things promised, but had seen them far
ahead and hailed them, and confessed themselves no
14 more than strangers or passing travellers on earth. Those
who use such language show plainly that they are looking
15 for a country of their own. If their hearts had been in the
country they had left, they could have found opportunity
16 to return. Instead, we find them longing for a better
country—I mean, the heavenly one. That is why God is
not ashamed to be called their God; for he has a city
ready for them.

✶ This new section on faith arises out of the previous verses,
10: 37–39, and out of the Habakkuk passage. It is a list of
biblical great men, all of whom, our writer argues, were men
with 'faith to make life their own'.

Our writer probably bases the first part of the list on the
first part of the list of 'famous men' in Ecclus. 44–50. From
Noah to Moses, he lists the same names in the same order,
though with the addition of Abel and Joseph, who do not
appear in the list in Ecclesiasticus.

1. First, a double definition of faith. Faith points to the
future (*gives substance to our hopes*) and to the heavenly

realities in the present time (*makes us certain of realities we do not see*). It thus looks to a heaven which is both in the future and in the present: in the future from the point of view of men awaiting the second coming, but also a present reality unseen by them. In the following list the future aspect predominates, so that 'faith' is closely related to perseverance and endurance.

2. The nature of this verse should be noted. It is not a statement of accepted fact—the Old Testament explicitly ascribes *faith* to very few of the following heroes. It is a statement of our writer's view: that the heroism of these men was actually caused by their faith. The following examples are brought in to support this view: verse 3 can be imagined to begin 'It is by faith that...' and the following verses to begin 'It was by faith that...'

3. This is really an extension of verse 1. Our faith that God created the world is an example of the second definition, that faith is the certainty 'of realities we do not see'.

4. The list begins here with *Abel* (Gen. 4: 2–11). The argument depends on the word *goodness*, which ought to be translated *righteousness*, for it is a reference to 10: 38. The argument then runs: God approved his offerings, which shows that he was *righteous*; and since it is 'by faith that my righteous servant shall find life' (10: 38), Abel must have had faith.

he continued to speak after his death (see Gen. 4: 10). After Cain had murdered him, Abel's blood, God said, 'cried to him from the ground', i.e. called for justice. The idea is that Abel's blood (which our writer identifies with Abel himself) in calling for justice declared his own righteousness.

5. *Enoch* (Gen. 5: 24, Ecclus. 44: 16). Here also *faith* has to be proved. Enoch was taken to heaven without death because *he pleased God* (which is stated in the LXX version of Gen. 5: 24): and this, our writer asserts, presupposes *faith*.

6. An argument to support the assertion. Anyone who seeks fellowship with God must obviously believe in his existence and goodwill.

he exists...he rewards: corresponding to the two aspects of faith (verse 1)—'realities we do not see' and 'substance to our hopes'.

7. *Noah* (Ecclus. 44: 17). Gen. 6: 9 (LXX) calls him 'a righteous man...pleasing to God': these qualities presuppose faith (cf. Abel and Enoch), but Noah's acts also demonstrate it. He could not see the *unseen future* (note how this combines both aspects of faith), but believed God's warning and acted upon it. He *put the whole world in the wrong* because he alone was in the right.

made good his claim. Better in the original, 'he became heir'. The reference is to God's declaration in Genesis 7: 1, 'thee have I seen righteous before me', before the flood began. Noah had shown faith in building the ark, and now was declared righteous by God.

8. *Abraham* (Ecclus. 44: 19). Abraham is the great example of faith in Galatians 3 and Romans 4: also Acts 7: 2ff. and James 2: 21ff. Our writer gives four examples of his faith: First, he *left home without knowing where he was to go*, but believing God's promise of a *land destined for himself and his heirs* (Genesis 12: 1 and 2).

9, 10. Secondly, he lived as a wandering shepherd, as did his son and grandson. Here the writer turns the Old Testament to his own purpose. Although Abraham reached the promised land, he only lived *in tents*, and never settled in one place: the fact that he built no city shows that he was looking forward to the heavenly city. Compare chapter 3, where scripture is held to show that the *rest* meant not Canaan but heaven.

the city with firm foundations is a leading idea of the last three chapters. It is mentioned in 11: 16 and 13: 14 and defined in 12: 22 as *heavenly Jerusalem*. It has the same relationship to the earthly city as the heavenly sanctuary to the Tent.

whose architect and builder is God. Compare 8: 2, 'the tent pitched by the Lord and not by man'.

11, 12. *Sarah.* This verse may also be translated with Abraham as the subject of the sentence: 'By faith he received strength to beget a child upon Sarah herself, even though she was past the age, because he judged...' etc. It thus becomes the third example of Abraham's faith. It is based on the story in Gen. 15: 1–6, where God promised Abraham a son, 'and he believed in the Lord' (Gen. 15: 6a).

If Sarah is left as subject, the argument is of the same type as for Enoch: she must have had faith, or she could not have had the child.

12. *one as good as dead*: because beyond the age of begetting children. The rest of the verse quotes Gen. 22: 17.

13–16. A summary of the preceding examples; in fact most of the details refer only to Abraham, but the general idea fits all.

13. *All these died in faith*. Not Enoch, strictly. The point is that they never possessed *the things promised* in their lifetime, but looked to the future. What they saw *far ahead* was the perfection (11: 40) brought by Jesus—the 'good things' of which he is high priest (9: 11).

confessed themselves strangers or passing travellers on earth. Literally true of the four named after verse 8, but figuratively of the first three also. An allusion to Abraham's words in Gen. 23: 4, 'I am a stranger and a sojourner with you.'

Those who use such language: the generalized 'those' is probably meant to include David, who says in 1 Chron. 29: 15, 'For we are strangers before thee, and sojourners, as all our fathers were: our days on the earth are as a shadow, and there is no abiding' (cf. Ps. 39: 12).

15. *in the country they had left*. Abraham and Jacob had both left their native land: the fact that they never returned shows that they were looking to the future.

16. The writer asserts that they were in fact longing for the heavenly country. And God *has a city ready for them*: their desire for it shows they are worthy of him, so that he is *not ashamed to be called their God*. The reference is to the declaration to Moses in Exodus 3: 6, 'I am the God of your father, the God of Abraham, the God of Isaac, and the God of Jacob.'

The idea of a future country with a future city is a further part of the writer's 'desert typology' (see p. 46). Israel was travelling to the promised land, in which the city of Jerusalem would become its centre: and now Christians are travelling through this life to the heavenly country, where 'heavenly Jerusalem' (12: 22) will be their city. ✳

FAITH: ABRAHAM TO RAHAB

17 By faith Abraham, when the test came, offered up Isaac: he had received the promises, and yet he was on the point

18 of offering his only son, of whom he had been told, 'Through the line of Isaac your posterity shall be traced.'

19 For he reckoned that God had power even to raise from the dead—and from the dead, he did, in a sense, receive him back.

20 By faith Isaac blessed Jacob and Esau and spoke of

21 things to come. By faith Jacob, as he was dying, blessed each of Joseph's sons, and worshipped God, leaning on the

22 top of his staff. By faith Joseph, at the end of his life, spoke of the departure of Israel from Egypt, and instructed them what to do with his bones.

23 By faith, when Moses was born, his parents hid him for three months, because they saw what a fine child he

24 was; they were not afraid of the king's edict. By faith Moses, when he grew up, refused to be called the son of

25 Pharoah's daughter, preferring to suffer hardship with the people of God rather than enjoy the transient pleasures of

26 sin. He considered the stigma that rests on God's Anointed greater wealth than the treasures of Egypt, for his eyes

27 were fixed upon the coming day of recompense. By faith he left Egypt, and not because he feared the king's

anger; for he was resolute, as one who saw the invisible God.

By faith he celebrated the Passover and sprinkled the 28 blood, so that the destroying angel might not touch the first-born of Israel. By faith they crossed the Red Sea as 29 though it were dry land, whereas the Egyptians, when they attempted the crossing, were drowned.

By faith the walls of Jericho fell down after they had 30 been encircled on seven successive days. By faith the 31 prostitute Rahab escaped the doom of the unbelievers, because she had given the spies a kindly welcome.

✼ 17–19. *Abraham* (Gen. 22: 1–18). The list is resumed with Abraham's fourth act of faith: he was willing to obey the command to kill Isaac despite the fact that only *through the line of Isaac* could God's promise of many descendants be kept. This was faith in God's promises despite all appearances: our writer argues that it was faith in God's power to restore Isaac to life.

17. *when the test came*. An allusion to Gen. 22: 1, 'After these things God tested Abraham' (R.S.V.).

he had received the promises: in the sense that he had had Isaac, through whom the promises would be fulfilled.

19. The striking comment that Isaac's escape from death was almost a resurrection emphasizes the power of God to reward the faithful even through extreme sufferings. It anticipates the resurrection theme later in the chapter.

20–22. *Isaac, Jacob, Joseph*. The three next descendants of Abraham all made, at the end of their lives, powerful predictions about future events, thus showing that they had faith in the unseen future workings of God.

20. *Isaac* (Gen. 27: 27–41, Ecclus. 44: 22). When Jacob stole Esau's blessing, Isaac prophesied the future of both his sons: Jacob would be powerful and prosper, Esau would live by his sword.

21. *Jacob* (Gen. 48: 1–20, Ecclus. 44: 23). Jacob on his deathbed blessed Ephraim and Manasseh and prophesied that their descendants would be many. His faith looked ahead to his grandsons' future.

and worshipped God, leaning on the top of his staff: a quotation from Gen. 47: 31 in the Septuagint. The Hebrew original is 'bowed himself upon the bed's head' and refers to Jacob reclining in weakness on his deathbed. The Greek version took the verb to mean 'bow in worship', and mistranslated 'bed' as 'staff', resulting in the words our writer quotes.

Our writer mistakes the original context of the words: they are not part of Jacob's blessing of Ephraim and Manasseh, but of the story before it. It is hard to see why he quotes it at all: perhaps because it shows that Jacob worshipped God as he looked into the future, and therefore that he had faith.

22. *Joseph* (Gen. 50: 22–26) on his deathbed foresaw the Exodus and the future of his own remains.

23–29. *Moses* (Ecclus. 45: 1). Five examples of faith are drawn from Moses' career as leader of Israel.

23. First example (Exod. 1: 15 — 2: 2). Moses' parents disobey the Pharaoh's order that male Israelite babies must be put to death. Their fearlessness shows that they had faith that God would save Moses in some way.

24–26. Second example (Exod. 2: 11–15). Moses had been brought up in the Egyptian court. By killing an Egyptian who was striking an Israelite, he identified himself with his own people, came under Pharaoh's displeasure, and fled the country (Exod. 2: 15). In this sense he *refused to be called the son of Pharaoh's daughter*.

25, 26. Moses' decision is described in two antitheses. He chose *hardship with the people of God* and *the stigma that rests on God's Anointed* (i.e. Israel): he rejected *the transient pleasures of sin*—the comfort of the court, which was sinful because hostile to God's people—and *the treasures of Egypt*—the riches of the court.

26. *the stigma that rests on God's Anointed*: an allusion to

Ps. 89: 50f., referring to the sufferings of David and Israel. Our writer means that Moses chose sufferings with Israel: perhaps he also thinks of Moses as in a sense choosing suffering with Christ, the real *God's Anointed*.

27. Third example. This verse probably refers not to the Exodus, but to Moses' flight after killing the Egyptian (Exod. 2: 15): it then follows directly upon the previous example. Hence the reference to Moses' fear, mentioned in Exod. 2: 14.

not because he feared the king's anger. In Exodus 2: 14 Moses is indeed afraid, though his flight in verse 15 is not explicitly connected with fear. Our writer is saying, 'Moses was afraid, but that was not his real motive for flight (in fact he was resolute, as the following events showed): his real reason was his faith.' Philo argued that Moses was not running away, but withdrawing for a while before returning to save Israel.

as one who saw the invisible God. This echoes 11: 1. Moses was as certain of unseen realities as if he had actually seen the unseen God. Or, since Moses is said on later occasions to have seen God (Exod. 24: 11, Deut. 34: 10), the sense may be *as a man who did later see God.*

28. Fourth example (Exod. 12: 21–28). Moses obeyed God's commands about the Passover, in faith that the Israelite first-born would be spared. This and the next two items are all about great miracles of deliverance, in which there was faith in the unseen power of God to keep his promise of salvation. In all three cases the people concerned believed God's promise and showed their faith by carrying out his instructions, like Noah in verse 7.

29. Fifth example (Exod. 14: 21–29). The crossing of the Red Sea, by the people under Moses' leadership.

30. (Josh. 6: 1–21). The fall of Jericho before the people under Joshua's leadership. Here the faith consisted in carrying out God's instructions to march round the city on the seven successive days.

31. (Josh. 6: 22–25). Only Rahab and her family were spared of the people of Jericho. She had concealed the two

Israelite spies who had previously entered the city (Josh. 2: 1–21), explaining (verses 8–11) that she knew that the Israelites' God was going to give the land of Canaan to them. She is thus an evident example of faith; also of hospitality, to which the readers are exhorted (see the commands to 'show hospitality' and 'remember those in prison' in 13: 2 and 3). Her inclusion in a list of Old Testament heroes may surprise us, but she is praised in several rabbinic works, and by Josephus, the first-century Jewish scholar. In the New Testament, in James 2: 25, 26, she is made an example of faith by good deeds. It seems likely that our writer was familiar with this view of her. *

FAITH: HEROES AND MARTYRS

32 Need I say more? Time is too short for me to tell the stories of Gideon, Barak, Samson, and Jephthah, of David
33 and Samuel and the prophets. Through faith they overthrew kingdoms, established justice, saw God's promises
34 fulfilled. They muzzled ravening lions, quenched the fury of fire, escaped death by the sword. Their weakness was turned to strength, they grew powerful in war, they
35 put foreign armies to rout. Women received back their dead raised to life. Others were tortured to death, dis-
36 daining release, to win a better resurrection. Others, again, had to face jeers and flogging, even fetters and
37 prison bars. They were stoned, they were sawn in two, they were put to the sword, they went about dressed in skins of sheep or goats, in poverty, distress, and misery.
38 They were too good for this world. They were refugees in deserts and on the hills, hiding in caves and holes in the
39 ground. These also, one and all, are commemorated for their faith; and yet they did not enter upon the promised

inheritance, because, with us in mind, God had made a 40
better plan, that only in company with us should they
reach their perfection.

✶ The list now becomes only names, and then unnamed
incidents. The chronology is abandoned, and though many
of the incidents are identifiable, they become in effect general
examples. As a result, the heroes seem to increase to a great
company, and to reach nearer to the readers' own time. A new
aspect of faith—endurance under persecution—becomes
central. The style, by its short, grouped phrases, assists in
producing a powerful sense of climax.

32. *Gideon, Barak, Samson, and Jephthah* (Judg. chapters
6 — 8, chapter 4, chapters 13 — 16, and chapter 11, respectively): four of the 'judges' who ruled Israel during the period
from Joshua to the monarchy. All four saved Israel from
neighbouring enemies, in circumstances requiring faith in
God's promises to them, and in extraordinary ways.

David, Samuel, and the prophets. David is probably included
not as king of Israel but as conqueror of the Philistines: hence
his place in the list with the 'judges'. Samuel was the last
'judge' (1 Sam. 7: 15) and the first of the great named
prophets (1 Sam. 3: 20), so that his name leads naturally to
the prophets in general.

33–34. Each sentence is a group of three phrases: the pace
of the writing quickens.

33. Probably intended to refer to the men just named, all
of whom overthrew Israel's enemies (even Samuel, in a
sense—e.g. his part in the defeat of the Philistines at Mizpah,
1 Sam. 7: 5–13), ruled the nation, and so had God's promises
of victory, made to them in times of crisis, fulfilled.

33 *b*. From this point incidents are named as though they
were general classes of faithful acts, though some are single
events which we can identify. Some are about the prophets, as
verse 32 implies, but not all. Some refer to Late Jewish books
current in the writer's time, but not subsequently included

in the Bible as we have it. Increasingly they become examples of faith under persecution.

muzzled ravening lions. Samson (Judg. 14: 6), David (1 Sam. 17: 36), and Daniel (Dan. 6: 22: our writer quotes this from the LXX).

quenched the fury of fire. Shadrach, Meshach and Abednego (Dan. 3), in the burning fiery furnace.

escaped death by the sword: possibly Daniel (Dan. 2: 13) in particular, in view of the previous phrases.

34. This applies to many events in Israel's history, but it may refer particularly to the period of the Maccabean revolt, since the next verse does so. This revolt, named after its hero Judas Maccabaeus and his family, is narrated in the two apocryphal Books of the Maccabees. It began in 167 B.C., and led to a period of Jewish independence.

35. The verse is an antithesis. The first half refers to the restoring to life of two children, by Elijah (1 Kings 17: 22) and Elisha (2 Kings 4: 34), at the request of their mothers. The second refers to the seven sons of a mother, who were tortured to death during the Maccabean revolt (2 Macc. 7). The mother saw them killed, but encouraged one of them with the hope that 'in the mercy of God I may receive thee again with thy brethren' (2 Macc. 7: 29). This passage colours our writer's language in both parts of the verse.

Others were tortured to death... A summary of 2 Macc. 7. The sons were tortured for refusing to break the Law of Moses. The second in particular refused an offer of release, and affirmed that God would raise them all *to life*.

a better resurrection. In the life to come, and so *better* than the resurrection of the mothers' sons by Elijah and Elisha, which was only a return to earthly life.

36. *jeers and flogging.* Both words occur in 2 Macc. 7, and the writer probably takes them from there, though he applies them in a general way (*Others, again...*).

fetters and prison bars. General, but perhaps specially referring to Jeremiah the prophet, who was put in the stocks (Jer. 20:

2) and later in prison (Jer. 37, 38) for his persistence in prophesying the doom of Israel. This would connect with the next verse—

37. *they were sawn in two.* It was a traditional belief in Late Judaism, found in the *Ascension of Isaiah* (a Jewish book of the second century A.D.) that the prophet Isaiah had been martyred in this way under Manasseh, the idolatrous king of Judah who 'shed innocent blood very much' during his reign (2 Kings 21: 16).

they were put to the sword. Probably an echo of Elijah's words in 1 Kings 19: 10, referring to Jezebel's killing of the prophets (1 Kings 18: 4, 13), and of the death of the prophet Uriah at the order of Jehoiakim (Jer. 26: 23).

they went about dressed in skins of sheep or goats. According to the *Ascension of Isaiah*, Isaiah's companions in the desert, who were prophets, wore garments of hair. There may also be a reference to Elijah's 'garment of haircloth' (2 Kings 1: 8, R.S.V.)

poverty, distress, and misery. Note the effective ending produced by this succession of almost synonymous nouns.

38. They were too good for this world: and supremely worthy of the 'age to come'.

deserts...hills...caves...holes. The Maccabees were 'wandering in the mountains and in the caves' (2 Macc. 10: 6) in the early stages of their revolt.

39. *These...are commemorated for their faith*: the writer repeats the argument of the whole preceding list—'it is for their faith that all these are commemorated'—and then points out that for all of them it was an unfulfilled faith. He is back to the contrast of the Old and New Covenants. *They did not enter upon the promised inheritance*: 'the way into the sanctuary remained unrevealed' (9: 8). But when the New did come, both they and Christians entered upon it.

and yet they did not enter. The unexpected negative is a very rhetorical touch—a sudden apparent anticlimax, making the following climax (12: 1, 2) even more effective.

40. *with us in mind*: bringing the argument back to the readers.

a better plan: to 'bring many sons to glory' (2: 10) through Jesus.

reach their perfection. The 'men of old' could not attain perfection until Christ had 'by one offering perfected for all time those who are consecrated' (10: 14). Christ's work being done, the 'men of old' can receive their reward, *in company with us*. See the note on 12: 23, p. 127. ✱

FAITH: JESUS THE PIONEER AND PERFECTER

12 And what of ourselves? With all these witnesses to faith around us like a cloud, we must throw off every encumbrance, every sin to which we cling, and run with resolu-
2 tion the race for which we are entered, our eyes fixed on Jesus, on whom faith depends from start to finish: Jesus who, for the sake of the joy that lay ahead of him, endured the cross, making light of its disgrace, and has taken his seat at the right hand of the throne of God.

✱ Our writer has a fertile mind for appropriate metaphors. He sees the Christian life as movement towards a goal: hence the analogy of Israel journeying to the promised land. Here he uses the image of a race, with runners stripped and resolute.

1. *witnesses to faith*. The scriptures witnessed to their faith ('they are commemorated for their faith', 11: 39), and so they can be called witnesses to the power of faith. But the phrase *around us like a cloud* suggests the additional sense of 'spectators', watching the race.

every encumbrance, every sin. The runners in the games were stripped completely: Christians must be stripped of their sins.

sin to which we cling or (N.E.B. footnote) *clinging sin* or *sin which all too readily distracts us*. The first version fits the race metaphor least well—the runners strip because their clothes impede them, not because they cling to their clothes. The third version occurs in the earliest manuscript, fits the metaphor best, and is probably the original.

resolution: the same Greek word as 'endurance' (10: 36) and 'resolute' (of Moses, 11: 27).

for which we are entered: better translated 'that lies ahead of us', so as to bring out the correspondence with the 'joy that lay before him' in verse 2—we run the same race that Jesus did. The same Greek word is used in both places.

2. *our eyes fixed on Jesus*: who has arrived at the goal before us.

on whom faith depends from start to finish: literally, and preferably, 'the pioneer and perfecter of faith' (or 'the starter and finisher of faith'). *Faith* does not mean Jesus' gift of faith to us, but his own faith (cf. 'faithful as their high priest', 2: 17; 'faithful as a son', 3: 6). He is the supreme example of faith, and the climax of the list of heroes. 'Pioneer' means that Jesus was the first man to reach 'perfection', and thus opened the path for others to follow. 'Perfecter' means that he was the first man to achieve perfect faith.

The rest of verse 2 shows the effect of Jesus' faith: by it he looked to his heavenly goal, withstood suffering, and reached heaven.

endured: the same word as in verse 1 ('resolution'): Jesus showed the virtues his followers can now copy.

its disgrace: the disgrace of being treated as a sinner, and of suffering a criminal's death.

and has taken his seat... A last quotation from Ps. 110: 4. The perfect tense of the verb emphasizes Jesus' present state, as our priest seated in heaven.

12: 2 shows with 10: 12 and 1: 3 the pattern of death and exaltation, suffering and glory, offering and entering, which in its various forms is general in the New Testament writers' thought about Jesus' death and vindication. Cf. especially Phil. 2: 8, 9 'he humbled himself, and in obedience accepted even death—death on a cross. Therefore God raised him to the heights and bestowed upon him the name above all names, that at the name of Jesus every knee should bow...' ✳

ACCEPT SUFFERING

3 Think of him who submitted to such opposition from sinners: that will help you not to lose heart and grow faint.
4 In your struggle against sin, you have not yet resisted to
5 the point of shedding your blood. You have forgotten the text of Scripture which addresses you as sons and appeals to you in these words:

'My son, do not think lightly of the Lord's discipline, Nor lose heart when he corrects you;
6 For the Lord disciplines those whom he loves; He lays the rod on every son whom he acknowledges.'

7 You must endure it as discipline: God is treating you as sons. Can anyone be a son, who is not disciplined by his
8 father? If you escape the discipline in which all sons
9 share, you must be bastards and no true sons. Again, we paid due respect to the earthly fathers who disciplined us; should we not submit even more readily to our spiritual
10 Father, and so attain life? They disciplined us for this short life according to their lights; but he does so for our
11 true welfare, so that we may share his holiness. Discipline, no doubt, is never pleasant; at the time it seems painful, but in the end it yields for those who have been trained by it the peaceful harvest of an honest life.

✳ 3. The emphasis has just been on the end product of Jesus' faith: now it turns to his endurance while still going through his sufferings. The readers, in their present hardships, may be more encouraged by the thought of Jesus in his sufferings than by the thought of his glory. Our writer offers five points of encouragement, of which this is the first.

such opposition: literally 'contradiction', i.e. verbal attack, like the false accusations and mockery of Jesus. The readers are under pressure by words—perhaps the attempts to turn them to Judaism.

4. Second point. A contrast with Jesus: the readers have not had to suffer anything like as seriously as he did.

struggle against sin: the sin of their opponents: perhaps also their own sin which has weakened their opposition.

you have not yet resisted...is often thought to show that they had not been subject to official persecution with violence. If the letter was to Rome, this would indicate a date before Nero's persecution in A.D. 64.

5–8. Third point: suffering, being God's discipline, actually proves that they are his sons. The writer appeals to scripture. Quotation: Prov. 3: 11, 12, the words of the writer to his 'son'. Application: God speaking to the readers (*addresses you, appeals to you*). Only the context is interpreted, not the content.

addresses you as sons. Because God is the author of scripture, he can be taken as the speaker of the words *My son*. In applying the quotation to the readers, our writer can therefore say that God is addressing them as sons.

The proverb argues that God's discipline is a sign both of God's love and of the sufferer's sonship. It does not state what the *discipline* is, but doubtless refers to suffering and hardship in this world.

he lays the rod on: LXX only; the Hebrew is 'as a father does to...' Our writer is thinking of *flogging* (11: 36) and similar sufferings: perhaps also of Jesus' floggings between his arrest and execution (cf. Mark 15: 15).

7, 8. The writer presses the point of the proverb. All sons are disciplined by their father: not to be disciplined would show that they were not real sons at all.

9, 10. Fourth point: they accepted their own fathers' discipline, which was designed *for this short life* and guided by their fathers' limited wisdom (*according to their lights*): they should *even more readily* accept God's which is designed *for our true welfare*, and (implicitly) guided by his unlimited wisdom.

11. Fifth point: discipline is easier to bear if its purpose is remembered—*an honest life*. The end product is pleasant, even if the process is not. ✲

CONQUER YOUR WEAKNESSES

12 Come, then, stiffen your drooping arms and shaking knees,
13 and keep your steps from wavering. Then the disabled limb will not be put out of joint, but regain its former powers.

14 Aim at peace with all men, and a holy life, for without
15 that no one will see the Lord. See to it that there is no one among you who forfeits the grace of God, no bitter,
16 noxious weed growing up to poison the whole, no
17 immoral person, no one worldly-minded like Esau. He sold his birthright for a single meal, and you know that although he wanted afterwards to claim the blessing, he was rejected; for he found no way open for second thoughts, although he strove, to the point of tears, to find one.

✲ Notice our writer's method of encouragement, used here and in the similar passages 3: 1–12 and 10: 32–39. He asks his readers to consider something and then urges them to act upon it.

12, 13. A return to the athletic metaphor of verse 1: a loose quotation of Isa. 35:3 and of Prov. 4: 26.

Then the disabled limb...The readers are already weakened: if they act now they can recover, but otherwise they will get worse.

14. *Aim at peace with all men*: probably not meant here as a general command, but aimed at the readers' situation. *Peace* is threatened by hostility from outside the church, but from within also, to judge from the next verses.

a holy life, for without that no one will see the Lord. If this is aimed at the readers' particular situation, it is the first hint of a fresh aspect of their weakness. It seems to presuppose that some of them were not sufficiently aware of the connection between religion and morality—a connection long known to Judaism but not to some other religions. It is thus an indication that the readers were Gentiles.

see the Lord: at his second coming.

15–17. These verses return to the warning of 6: 4ff. about the impossibility of repentance after apostasy.

15. *See to it*...Compare the command in 3: 12.

forfeits the grace of God: by apostasy, as the next phrase indicates.

no bitter, noxious weed...poison the whole. Quoted from Deut. 29: 18 (LXX): Moses' warning that apostasy might grow and contaminate Israel once they had settled in Canaan.

no immoral person: the Greek means specifically sexual immorality: though, in view of the context, it may have the metaphorical meaning sometimes used in the Old Testament (e.g. Judg. 2: 17) of worshipping other gods.

16. *no one worldly-minded like Esau*: i.e. attached to this life and neglectful of the world to come.

17. Esau's worldly-mindedness is shown by the two incidents now mentioned by our writer.

(*a*) Gen. 25: 29–34 tells how Esau, under stress of physical exhaustion, gave his younger brother Jacob his birthright (the position and privileges of the eldest son) in exchange for a meal. Our writer is thinking of his readers' temptation under stress to give up their Christian heritage.

(*b*) Gen. 27 tells how Jacob tricked his father Isaac into giving him the eldest son's blessing (part of the birthright, in fact) properly due to Esau. On discovering this, Esau *wanted to claim the blessing*, but as it had been given to Jacob, and could not be reversed, his request could not be granted—*he was rejected*, in that sense.

Our writer has taken these two stories to be causally connected; and though this is not stated in Genesis, it is a natural interpretation. The birthright entailed the blessing; and Esau, who was to blame for losing the first, lost the second and could not get it back.

he found no way open for second thoughts. Isaac could not alter the situation, because the blessing was irrevocably Jacob's. Esau might be said to have had *second thoughts*—repented— about having previously sold his birthright. Our writer uses Esau as an example to his readers, who are in danger of his sin and its consequences. If they give up their birthright they will lose their blessing. That is, if they let their Christian sonship go, by apostasy, they will lose their heavenly salvation.

In the Genesis story the blessing is irrevocable because of the ancient view that a blessing is a word that actually brings about the events it speaks of. Therefore, once it is said, the events are set in motion, and the blessing cannot be unsaid and then said for someone else. ✳

MOUNT SINAI AND MOUNT ZION

18 Remember where you stand: not before the palpable, blazing fire of Sinai, with the darkness, gloom, and
19 whirlwind, the trumpet-blast and the oracular voice,
20 which they heard, and begged to hear no more; for they could not bear the command, 'If even an animal touches
21 the mountain, it must be stoned.' So appalling was the sight, that Moses said, 'I shudder with fear.'

No, you stand before Mount Zion and the city of the 22
living God, heavenly Jerusalem, before myriads of
angels, the full concourse and assembly of the first-born 23
citizens of heaven, and God the judge of all, and the
spirits of good men made perfect, and Jesus the mediator 24
of a new covenant, whose sprinkled blood has better
things to tell than the blood of Abel. See that you do not 25
refuse to hear the voice that speaks. Those who refused to
hear the oracle speaking on earth found no escape; still
less shall we escape if we refuse to hear the One who
speaks from heaven. Then indeed his voice shook the 26
earth, but now he has promised, 'Yet once again I will
shake not earth alone, but the heavens also.' The words 27
'once again'—and only once—imply that the shaking of
these created things means their removal, and then what
is not shaken will remain. The kingdom we are given is 28
unshakable; let us therefore give thanks to God, and so
worship him as he would be worshipped, with reverence
and awe; for our God is a devouring fire.   29

✻ This section develops from the warning in verses 15–17. It
returns to the method of warning previously used in 2: 1–4
and 10: 28–31. If disobedience under the Old Covenant
brought inescapable punishment, how much more will it do so
under the New! But here the thing disobeyed is not the Law,
but God's voice itself, as it spoke at Sinai and now speaks
from the heavenly mount Zion.

18–21. A description of the terrible signs of God's presence
at Sinai, where the Old Covenant was made. Most of the
details are loosely quoted from Exod. 19 and 20 (the Sinai
story) and from Deut. 4 and 5 (Moses' retelling of the story
forty years later).

18. *where you stand*: The verb means literally 'approach'

(see note on 4: 16): it echoes Deut. 4: 11, 'ye came near and stood under the mountain'. It connotes the worshipper's right to draw near, his 'standing' with God: so the N.E.B. translation well expresses the purpose of the paragraph—to remind the readers *where they stand* in relationship to God. They belong to the New Covenant, not the Old.

19. *the oracular voice*. The voice of God: quoted from Deut. 4: 12. The people were terrified at the signs of God's presence and his speaking in the thunder.

and begged to hear no more: The people would have God address only Moses, not themselves—'let not God speak to us, lest we die' (Exod. 20: 19). Thus they 'refused to hear him' (verse 25).

20. *they could not bear the command*...In the Exodus account, the only word which God had said to them before they *begged to hear no more* was the command to keep away from the mountain, on pain of death (Exod. 19: 12, 13). So our writer identifies this command with the utterance of the voice which terrified them.

'*If even an animal*...' Exod. 19: 13, quoted freely. The sternness of the command is shown by the fact that its threat extends even to animals.

'*I shudder with fear.*' Deut. 9: 19, quoted freely.

22–24. A description of the 'New Sinai', the meeting-place of God and his New Covenant people. It is heaven itself, like the 'real tent' of chapters 8 — 10. It is better than the old Sinai because it is heavenly, not earthly, and glorious, not terrible. But there is a further contrast: it is not called the 'heavenly Sinai', but the *heavenly Jerusalem*, because it is not the place from which they are setting out, but the end at which they are arriving.

22. *you stand before*. For the meaning, see note on 12: 18. What is the tense? The Greek says 'you have approached' (perfect tense), meaning that they are already there. So it is a present reality, as though they are at the foot of the mount: they already belong to heaven, and have access there in

126

Christ, even though they will not enter it until his second coming.

Mount Zion: the stronghold in Jerusalem captured by David (2 Sam. 5: 7), and in later biblical writing synonymous with 'Jerusalem'.

the city of the living God. The Jews believed that God was above all earthly things, and yet was present in the Tent, and later in the temple in Jerusalem, in a special way. Thus in I Kings 8: 11 we read that when King Solomon dedicated the temple 'the glory of the Lord filled the house of the Lord', even though in verse 27 Solomon declares 'heaven and the heaven of heavens cannot contain thee'. Jerusalem thus became thought of as an earthly counterpart to heaven, and was used as an image of it, as in the next two words.

heavenly Jerusalem. In the same relationship to the earthly city as the heavenly tent to the earthly, 9: 24. A Late Jewish idea, found also in Gal. 4: 26 and Rev. 21.

23. *myriads of angels.* Perhaps suggested by Deut. 33: 2, 'The Lord came from Sinai...he came from the ten thousands (= myriads) of holy ones (= angels)'.

the first-born citizens of heaven: meaning perhaps men, but more probably, from the order of the phrases, the angels, *first-born* in that they were created before man.

God the judge of all: note the emphasis on judgement: a sign that this picture of Zion is meant as a warning as well as an encouragement.

the spirits of good men made perfect. The meaning is probably the 'men of old' (11: 2), who 'did not enter upon the inheritance' in their own time, but have now done so— presumably because Jesus has now entered heaven as their forerunner. The writer does not make this point clear, but he is likely to have had a consistent view of the matter: and this would suggest that he thought that once Jesus had entered heaven, all those who had looked forward in faith could do so after him. The phrase might also include Christians who had already died, and followed Jesus 'through the veil'.

A further distinction may be intended. Our writer may use the word *spirits* deliberately, meaning that the *good men* are awaiting the second coming when their bodies will be raised and glorified (cf. 6: 2, 'the resurrection of the dead'). In this case, even the spirits in heaven would be awaiting the second coming for the glorification of their complete humanity, body and spirit. Some such idea is present in, e.g., Rom. 8: 23, and became common Christian belief at a later date. But the brevity of this phrase makes it uncertain whether our writer is reflecting such a belief, or using current ideas not yet systematically related.

24. *Jesus the mediator of a new covenant*. Zion is the new Sinai, and so there is now a return to the language of *covenant*. Whereas the Old Covenant was mediated by the angels and Moses, the New is mediated by Jesus. It is a fitting description of Jesus at this final climax of the letter, since it sums up the various themes that have been discussed.

whose sprinkled blood. The context makes it most likely that the writer is here thinking specifically of the blood-sprinkling of Exod. 24: 3–8. (See note on 9: 19.)

has better things to tell than that of Abel: an echo of 11: 4. Jesus' blood signifies his sacrifice for sins and his covenant with those sprinkled with it (10: 22): in fact it signifies obedience, redemption, salvation—the whole work of 'bringing many sons to glory'. Abel's blood signifies rebellion, hatred, sin—all causes of Christ's work.

25. The 'New Sinai' has been described in such a way as to show its glory and grace, in contrast to the old Sinai's terrors. But now its glory is suddenly turned to a warning: to disobey at Zion will be far worse than to disobey at Sinai.

25. *refuse to hear the voice that speaks* (literally *him who speaks*, God). An abrupt return to verse 19, with the same verb ('begged to hear no more' ... 'refused to hear').

the oracle speaking on earth...the One who speaks from heaven. The real contrast, and the real point of the Sinai imagery.

There God spoke on earth, now he speaks from heaven: refusal to hear him now will be far more severely judged.

found no escape: since they all subsequently died in the wilderness (cf. 3: 17).

who speaks from heaven: God speaks in Jesus and all that his coming brings to pass—he 'has spoken to us in the Son' (1: 2).

26–29. An additional contrast: at Sinai God spoke, but not finally; in Jesus he has spoken his last word, and the present choice, of obedience or refusal, is the final choice.

26. *his voice shook the earth*. The Hebrew text of Exod. 19: 18 includes an earthquake, though the LXX omits it. But our writer may be thinking of other Old Testament passages about the earthquake at Sinai—e.g. Judg. 5: 5 (LXX):

> 'The mountains were shaken at the presence of the Lord,
> And Sinai at the presence of the God of Israel.' (C.T.)

but now he has promised: the following quotation is from Haggai 2: 6, where God promises to intervene and glorify the newly rebuilt temple. Application: God promises to intervene with the last Day. The words are slightly altered to emphasize *the heavens*, and so to argue that the final shaking will be of the entire creation.

27. *once again*: the writer makes it mean 'only once again', and argues that such a final shaking must mean the end of all *created things*.

these created things: the *earth* and the *heavens*—the latter in the sense of 1: 10, the created heavens, not 'heaven itself' (9:24).

what is not shaken will remain: which must mean 'heaven itself', the heavenly Jerusalem and all in it.

28. But the faithful have a part in *what is not shaken* (verse 27), and will therefore survive the 'removal of the created things'.

The kingdom. A common New Testament description of the destiny of Christians in heaven. It is a Jewish idea, and the main theme of Jesus' preaching, according to the first three Gospels. Our writer presupposes this idea, but does not elaborate it: God is king, Jesus at his right hand shares his kingdom, and Christians are 'given it'.

we are given. The tense has the double force noted in previous passages about salvation: we will enter the kingdom at the Parousia, but it is ours now in principle.

let us therefore give thanks to God, and so worship him...The proper response to such a gift. After so much about looking forward, the writer ends on the note of present salvation and present worship.

with reverence and awe: again, the writer's sense of God's holiness and transcendence.

29. *for our God is a devouring fire.* Quotation: Deut. 4: 24, about God's 'jealousy', i.e. his refusal to countenance idolatry. The 'fire' image occurred also in 6: 8 and 10: 27, of judgement, but here it also continues the Sinai imagery (see verse 18) and gives the paragraph greater unity. Our writer has given warm encouragement in verse 28, but in verse 29 he gives severity the last word. He presumably thinks his readers need it. ✻

LIVE AS CHRISTIANS SHOULD

13 Never cease to love your fellow-Christians.

2 Remember to show hospitality. There are some who, by so doing, have entertained angels without knowing it.

3 Remember those in prison as if you were there with them; and those who are being maltreated, for you like them are still in the world.

4 Marriage is honourable; let us all keep it so, and the marriage-bond inviolate; for God's judgement will fall on fornicators and adulterers.

5 Do not live for money; be content with what you have; for God himself has said, 'I will never leave you or
6 desert you'; and so we can take courage and say, 'The

Lord is my helper, I will not fear; what can man do to me?'

Remember your leaders, those who first spoke God's 7 message to you; and reflecting upon the outcome of their life and work, follow the example of their faith.

Jesus Christ is the same yesterday, today, and for ever. 8

✲ 1. Literally, *let brotherly love continue*: i.e. love within the Christian community. After the previous tremendous warning, the main purpose of the letter recedes from the writer's mind, for a little, and he writes more generally.

2. *Hospitality*, highly regarded by the Jews and in the ancient East generally, was specially important for the early Church, which was knit together by travellers like the apostles. Cf. Paul's words in his letter to Philemon, 'have a room ready for me' (Philem. 22).

entertained angels without knowing it. Abraham and Sarah entertained three travellers who turned out to be angels (Gen. 18), and several similar stories occur in the Old Testament and in other ancient literature.

3. Apparently the imprisonment and ill treatment of some of the readers' fellow-Christians is not only a thing of the past, as 10: 33, 34 might suggest.

for you like them are still in the world. Literally *in the body*. Not, probably, the 'body of Christians', but the physical body. The readers can sympathize with the maltreated because they also are liable to physical ill treatment. Note the emphasis on imaginative sympathy in this verse: cf. the sympathy of Christ (2: 18, 4: 15).

4. Better translated 'Let marriage be honoured, and the marriage-bond kept inviolate, by us all...' This could be an attack on either sexual promiscuity or ascetic rejection of marriage: but the end of the verse indicates the former.

5, 6. The writer knows that avarice can be a form of seeking security, and gives the best antidote by speaking of

131

their true security under the care of God. The quotations are from Josh. 1: 5, God's words of encouragement to Joshua, and Ps. 118: 6, where the Psalmist declares his trust in God.

7. *Remember your leaders*: not the present ones, but those of the past, who apparently brought them the gospel and stayed to become their leaders.

the outcome: the effect of their lives, seen in retrospect. Or, differently translated, 'the conclusion' (meaning their death, as in Wisd. of Solomon 2: 17).

follow the example of their faith. They too are 'men of faith' like the heroes of chapter 11.

8. The mention of the past leads to the thought that the readers follow the same Lord as their past leaders did. So the writer declares (as it can better be translated) *Jesus Christ is the same yesterday and today*—(then, extending it further) *yes, and for ever*. Then this changelessness of Christ reminds him of their temptation to change their allegiance, and he turns his attention to that once more. ✷

THE OLD SACRIFICES AND THE NEW

9 So do not be swept off your course by all sorts of outlandish teachings; it is good that our souls should gain their strength from the grace of God, and not from scruples about what we eat, which have never done any good to those who were governed by them.

10 Our altar is one from which the priests of the sacred
11 tent have no right to eat. As you know, those animals whose blood is brought as a sin-offering by the high priest into the sanctuary, have their bodies burnt outside
12 the camp, and therefore Jesus also suffered outside the
13 gate, to consecrate the people by his own blood. Let us then go to him outside the camp, bearing the stigma that

he bore. For here we have no permanent home, but we 14
are seekers after the city which is to come. Through Jesus, 15
then, let us continually offer up to God the sacrifice of
praise, that is, the tribute of lips which acknowledge his
name, and never forget to show kindness and to share 16
what you have with others; for such are the sacrifices
which God approves.

✻ This is an attack on false teachings: and though they have
not been mentioned before, it seems most likely that they are
all part of the same danger that elicited the letter. The paragraph is not a closely knit argument: one idea leads to another
by association, rather than by logical consequence.

9. *outlandish teachings*. If the false teachings were Jewish, it
may seem strange that a Jewish Christian should call them
'outlandish'. But there were new developments in Judaism,
like the false teaching attacked in Colossians (e.g. 'self-
mortification and angel-worship', Col. 2: 18), and the readers
might be under pressure from these. Or the adjective may
simply be a piece of rhetorical exaggeration.

scruples about what we eat: presumably a specially prominent
feature of the false teaching. Food regulations were a prominent part of Judaism, and of its sects. Our writer dismisses
them all as irrelevant: *the grace of God* is what matters.

The question of food regulations was an important one for
the church in New Testament times: particularly as Jews became Christians, and had to learn a new outlook on rules and
customs which they had always believed to be divine commands. Such matters are the subject of the apostles' debate in
Jerusalem, narrated in Acts 15, and of Paul's instructions to his
readers in 1 Cor. 8-10 and Rom. 14.

which have never done any good...A general reflection, with
the Jews in mind.

10. The Jews have no share in our sacrifice.
altar: meaning sacrificial system, as in 7: 13.

the priests of the sacred tent. Literally 'those who serve the tent', the Jews whose worship is bound to the earthly sanctuary.

have no right to eat. Much of the food offered in the Levitical sacrifices was eaten by the priests: so eating was an integral part of their sacrifices.

11. But our sacrifice was different, and eating has nothing to do with it. The writer might have located the difference in the spiritual nature of Christ's sacrifice: but he argues otherwise. Even in the old sacrifices, the sin-offerings were not eaten: on the Day of Atonement the bull and goat, once killed, were burned *outside the camp* (Lev. 16: 27). So Christ's sacrifice, which was like the Day of Atonement sacrifices, was not the sort that involves eating. And this shows that scruples about eating have no part in the Christian life.

12. There was even a visible sign that Jesus' sacrifice was of this kind—his death was *outside the camp* (since Golgotha was outside Jerusalem). This piece of argument is strictly inconsistent with the earlier, where Jesus' death corresponded to the killing of the animal (9: 12), for here it corresponds to the disposal of the animal's body. In fact this is an entirely separate argument based on the single point suggested by the phrase *outside the camp.*

13. The place of Jesus' death now suggests a further idea. It was a sign of his separation from Judaism; his death put him outside the Old Covenant. Christians must be outside it too.

bearing the stigma that he bore. The stigma of his condemnation as a blasphemer. Christians, like him, are the object of Jewish condemnation.

14. Another idea. Jesus left Jerusalem when he went to die: Christians are with him, outside the city. They do not need a *permanent home* (literally 'city') here, because they have the heavenly one.

Notice that here the heavenly city is no longer contrasted with Sinai, but with the earthly Jerusalem.

15, 16. The proper response of Christians is to worship God and live in the fellowship with others. The same double response was urged in 10: 22 and 10: 24f., and in 12: 28 and 13: 1. It is our writer's equivalent to Jesus's two commandments, to love God and love one's neighbour. This is Christian life, and 'scruples about what we eat' are irrelevant.

15. *Through Jesus*, who as our priest and ministrant is the mediator of our praise.

offer up to God the sacrifice of praise. The words allude to Lev. 7: 12, instructions about offering a sacrifice for a thanksgiving (the same Greek word as *praise*): and to the theme, found in several psalms, and developed in the Judaism of this period, of offering God the 'sacrifice of thanksgiving' (e.g. Ps. 50: 14). The fundamental activity of Christians towards God is praise for their salvation by Christ, offered through the praise of Christ the high priest.

the tribute of lips which acknowledge his name. To *acknowledge his name* is to acknowledge that his name is the name of the true god, i.e. that he is God. It thus means to worship him as God.

16. *kindness and sharing with others* are the practical expressions of Christian love. Like praise, they are *sacrifices which God approves*—inward offerings of the worshipper's own life. ✶

FINAL MESSAGES

Obey your leaders and defer to them; for they are 17 tireless in their concern for you, as men who must render an account. Let it be a happy task for them, and not pain and grief, for that would bring you no advantage.

Pray for us; for we are convinced that our conscience is 18 clear; our one desire is always to do what is right. All the 19 more earnestly I ask for your prayers, that I may be restored to you the sooner.

20 May the God of peace, who brought up from the dead our Lord Jesus, the great Shepherd of the sheep, by the
21 blood of the eternal covenant, make you perfect in all goodness so that you may do his will, and may he make of us what he would have us be through Jesus Christ, to whom be glory for ever and ever! Amen.

22 I beg you, brothers, bear with this exhortation; for it is
23 after all a short letter. I have news for you: our friend Timothy has been released; and if he comes in time he will be with me when I see you.

24 Greet all your leaders and all God's people. Greetings to you from our Italian friends.

25 God's grace be with you all!

✷ 17. *Obey your leaders*. These must be the present leaders, to whom greetings are sent in verse 24. The letter is not being sent, apparently, to the entire church, or the *leaders* would be among the readers. Perhaps the readers are one group, possibly meeting in a member's house (the situation in the Letter to Philemon), in a city where the different groups are under a common leadership. The leaders' authority is equalled by their devotion and their responsibility. They are presumably not in the particular danger that the readers are in, but are closely concerned in its effects. The readers are told to obey them: perhaps the writer knows that this would prevent them turning from Christianity. The *pain and grief* will then mean specifically the leaders' grief if the group does fall away.

18, 19. The first words that shed light on the writer's relationship to his readers. The tone is friendly but rather formal, and fits the austere tone of the whole letter.

18. Perhaps the writer's motives have been doubted. *Always* should possibly be translated 'for all parties'.

19. He may want to be with them in order to convince them of the purity of his motives.

restored suggests that he has been at their church before.

20, 21. A final blessing. Verse 20 is based on part of Isa. 63: 11 (LXX), 'who brought up out of the land the shepherd of the sheep'. This refers to God guiding Moses out of Egypt at the Exodus. Our writer applies it to God 'bringing up' Jesus out of death.

the God of peace: notice that the writer does not think of God only as the stern Judge: he has emphasized the sterner aspect because of the particular purpose of his letter.

brought up from the dead. The only reference in Hebrews to the raising of Jesus *from the dead. Brought up* may include both the resurrection and the ascension. The parallel between the Exodus, when God *brought up* Moses from Egypt, and the resurrection of Christ, became a prominent theme in Christian liturgy and hymnody.

the great Shepherd. Jesus takes the place of Moses: the writer inserts *great* into his quotation, perhaps to stress Jesus' superiority.

by the blood of the eternal covenant. The phrase echoes 'the blood of the covenant' in Exod. 24: 8 (already quoted in 9: 20). *Eternal covenant* occurs several times in the Old Testament, but our writer is probably thinking of such passages as Jer. 32: 40 and Ezek. 37: 26, which use it of the new covenant they there foretell.

The sense of the whole phrase is 'by Jesus' death, the sacrifice of the new covenant'. The word *by* seems to make Jesus' death the means of his resurrection, but this is probably due to the compression of the sentence, for the writer elsewhere treats Jesus' death as the ground or cause of his resurrection (e.g. 5: 8-10).

21. *to whom be glory*: may refer to the 'God of peace' or to *Jesus Christ.* Grammatically the latter is preferable, and, seeing that the writer applies such a passage as 1: 8, 'Thy throne, O God, is for ever and ever', to Jesus, it is quite consistent with the rest of the letter.

Amen. In Hebrew 'So be it!'—the traditional response to prayer.

22. *a short letter*: possibly the writer is rather optimistic about the staying power of his readers' minds.

23. *released*. The natural meaning is 'released from prison'. Timothy may well be the junior companion of Paul (e.g. Acts 16: 1–3), who would be a prominent man in the church both in the apostles' generation and the next. But it could be someone otherwise unknown to us.

Timothy has to travel first to the writer's place, and *if he comes in time* he will travel with the writer to visit them.

24. *all your leaders...all God's people*. See note on verse 17.

from our Italian friends. All that these words prove is that the writer and his readers have friends in common who come from Italy, and who are with the writer when he sends off the letter. They prove nothing about where he was writing from or to, though they are compatible with either place being Rome.

25. *God's grace be with you all!* The same greeting as Titus 3: 15, and similar to those at the end of Paul's letters. The form is Jewish: Peace be to you! (Judg. 6: 23); God be gracious to you! (Gen. 43: 29) (both R.S.V.).

✳　✳　✳　✳　✳　✳　✳　✳　✳　✳　✳　✳　✳

HEBREWS AND CHRISTIAN THOUGHT TODAY

We do not know what effect the letter had on its original readers. But it has had effects far beyond its writer's intentions, since it became part of the New Testament and therefore one of the authoritative sources of Christian thought. It has had direct effects upon its many subsequent readers, notably those Christian theologians whose thought it has deeply influenced. And it has had indirect effects upon many more, whose lives have been influenced by Christian language, art, ideas, and worship based on it. The familiar ideas of Christ as the 'full, final sacrifice' and as the heavenly priest, of Christians as God's people 'marching to the Promised Land', and of the

Christian life as a 'pilgrim's progress', all spring from Hebrews.

What special insights of Hebrews can most help our own understanding of Christianity? I suggest that the following five points are among the most important.

(a) *The idea of God.* Our writer shows how he thinks of God by his use of the title from Gen. 14: 'God Most High'. For him God is incomparably greater than man, whose proper attitude to God is worship and obedience. God is 'the living God', severe and unerring in judgement, but also 'our gracious God' who sent his Son to 'bring many sons to glory'. The latter aspect of God underlies the whole argument of the letter, even though the former (because of the letter's purpose) is more obvious. Either way, God is sovereign, to be worshipped 'with reverence and awe'.

This idea of God is fundamental to all true religion, and corresponds to the intellectual conviction that God, if he exists, must be great beyond human imagining. It balances the other fundamental idea, of God's nearness and indwelling presence in the world and in man—an idea which may weaken and impoverish our thought about God by making him too like ourselves. Hebrews can help us to hold the balance truly.

(b) *The humanity of Christ.* Hebrews teaches that Christ is divine: but more than any other New Testament letter it teaches that he is truly human. It uses his human name 'Jesus' where other writers would use titles like 'the Lord': it makes much of his sharing flesh and blood (2: 14), of his belonging to the 'sons of Abraham' (2: 16) and the tribe of Judah (7: 14), and of his resultant understanding and sympathy for men (2: 18; 4: 15). It mentions his earthly life many times—his preaching (2: 3), trials and sufferings (2: 10; 2: 18; 5: 8), prayers and tears (5: 7), faith and endurance (12: 2), death outside Jerusalem (13: 12), resurrection (13: 20) and ascension (4: 14; 6: 20). And it emphasizes the quality which runs through the whole life, of obedience to God's will, made perfect in death and leading to the proper human goal of God's presence.

Hebrews can therefore strengthen our understanding of the real humanity of Christ, and prevent us from thinking that he was God in human *form* but did not truly share human life with its limitations, pressures, trials, and decisions.

(*c*) *The work of Christ.* This is inseparable from the last point, since it is only because he becomes true man that the Son can bring about man's salvation. This inner necessity is argued in chapter 2—only a man can fulfil man's destiny and represent all men to God. That is why Jesus offers himself in obedience and death to God, and so enters God's presence as mankind's forerunner and representative. All this is presented by our writer in the language of sacrifice and priesthood. But notice that he himself supplies the key to that language, by explaining that the true sacrifice is obedience, and that the true priesthood is the representation of all men by the one perfect man.

Our writer also brings out admirably the unity of the different stages of Christ's work. He came into the world to obey God ('to do thy will, O God'), his life was a process of ever-deepening obedience culminating in his self-offering in death, and this led to his present 'pleading on our behalf'. Hebrews avoids that isolation of the cross from the earthly and the heavenly life of Jesus, which is found in some explanations of Christ's work: for at all stages Christ is fulfilling the destiny of man.

(*d*) *The Christian life.* Our writer sees this life in the light of the next. This is partly because he believes that this world will soon be brought to an end when Christ appears again, but also because he has such a strong sense of Christ's presence for us in heaven now. So for him the Christian life in this world is following in the steps of Jesus, looking forward to our future salvation, and sticking faithfully to our religion through trials and sufferings. But he does not despise this world, and in chapter 13 gives positive teaching about living in it.

Today many Christians rightly emphasize the need to live for God and man in this world, and at first sight Hebrews gives this view small encouragement: but in fact it offers it unexpected kinds of support. First, it offers a sense of proportion. However important this life is, it needs to be seen in the light of man's final destiny, which lies beyond it: and those who see it in that light may well live in it the more usefully and discerningly. Secondly, it offers hope. Anything done in this world suffers from man's ill-will and weakness, and from the limitations of time, place, and circumstances: we feel the imperfection of even the best we achieve. Hebrews points to the next life as the realm where our ultimate hopes may properly lie, and where perfection is to be found: and this can enable us to live and work for God in this world without despair.

(e) *Christianity and other religions.* Hebrews mentions no religions other than Judaism and Christianity, but its treatment of these two suggests how we should understand the wider question of Christianity and the other religions of the world. If, like most Christians, we believe that God and man do have some real contact in these religions, we can echo Hebrews and say that in them God speaks to men 'in fragmentary and varied fashion' (how much, and how clearly, it is for those concerned to judge): and that in these religions men do have a way to God, though it is a shadow of the real way. In Christ the real word is spoken and the real way opened: and this both fulfils and supersedes all religions. But, like Judaism, they do not simply come to an end. For they provide words and ideas by which Christ can be described and interpreted, and so positively enable men to understand him. They live on in the Christianity they have thus expanded and enriched: though to turn from Christianity to them would be to forsake the reality for the shadow.

HOW TO STUDY HEBREWS FURTHER

Here are some suggestions for further study of Hebrews. For the letter's background, the most important thing is to know the Old Testament better: the more we understand the relevant parts of it, the more we can appreciate our writer's use of it. For the letter itself (and for its background too) there are several commentaries of about the same size as this one, all of them useful: and two readily available larger and fuller ones are those of F. F. Bruce and H. W. Montefiore. There are also more general books on Hebrews, such as A. Nairne's *The Epistle of Priesthood*, on its thought, and A. Vanhoye's extremely helpful *A Structured Translation of the Epistle to the Hebrews*, which is a literal translation printed in such a way that the letter's structure of verbal links and echoes can be properly appreciated. And it is well worth reading the letter in the various translations now available. Indeed, reading the letter itself is most important of all: sometimes rapidly, to grasp the overall design, sometimes spending time over the details. Every reading will give fresh understanding, for Hebrews is a seemingly inexhaustible work, always offering something new, or something old in a new light.

INDEX

Aaron, 32, 46, 52, 64, 85

Abel, 107, 128

Abraham, 32, 45, 61, 62, 66, 131; his faith, 108, 109, 111

access to God, 49, 85, 98, 99

ages, this age, 18; the age to come, 59

Alexandria, centre of Hellenistic Judaism, 12, 83; Apollos, 11

altar (= sacrificial system), 73, 133

altar of incense, 84

angels, prominence in Hebrews, 20, 21; mediators of the Law, 20, 25; lower than Jesus, 22–4, 27, 32, 48, 50, 131

Apocrypha, 12

Apollos, possible author, 11, 25

apostasy (falling away), unforgivable, 58–60, 101–2

argument, typical examples of the writer's methods, 14, 22, 25, 29, 40, 41, 45, 55, 60, 66, 69, 74, 76, 90, 97, 101, 107, 128

ark of the covenant, 84–5

Ascension of Isaiah, 117

Assumption of Moses, 12

Atonement, Day of, 32, 64; *also* 51–2, 63, 65, 74, 76, 85, 92, 95

baptism, 56, 58, 99, 103

Barnabas, possible author, 9, 25; *Letter of Barnabas*, 10

blood, and expiation, 85; and covenant, 89–91, 137; sprinkling, 90, 99; of animals, 94; of Christ, 87, 99, 100; of Abel, 107, 128; of Jesus, 128

boldness (confidence), 49–50, 103–4

Bruce, F. F., commentary on Hebrews, 142

Canaan, *see* Promised Land

cherubim, 85

Christianity, and Judaism, 4, 5, 18; and other religions, 141; writer's

background, 11–12, 54–6; rudiments, 54–6

Christian art, 1, 31, 53, 138

Christian life in this world, 140–1

Christian liturgy and worship, 31, 137, 139

city, heavenly, 46, 109, 110, 127, 134

Clement of Alexandria, 2, 10, 11, 14

Clement of Rome, bishop, 6; letter to Corinthians (*I Clement*), 6, 8; possible author of Hebrews, 10

Colossae, possible destination, 7

contrasts, 13; old and new, 18; covenants, 81, 104; sacrifices, 76, 82, 86, 134; earth and heaven, 78–9, 87, 106, 134; outward and inward, 86, 94; men and angels, 30–2; *see also* superiority

copy, 79, 90–1

covenant, and promises, 79, 81; and sacrifices and sanctuary, 82–6; and death, 89–91; old and new covenants, 13, 46, 74, 80–1, 125–6, 128

creation, 13, 19

curtain (= veil), 84, 99; *see also* veil

David, 109, 113–14

day, of judgement, 110; *see also* Parousia

Dead Sea Scrolls, 7, 12, 53

death of Jesus, its effects, 31–2; a self-offering, 87; a sacrifice of obedience, 95–6

desert, Israel travelling forty years, 32; analogy with Christians, 38; 'desert typology', 46, 48, 110

Egypt, the exodus from, 39, 41, 112–13, 137

encouragement, passages of, 40, 48, 98, 102, 122

endurance, 104, 113, 119–21; *see also* faith

143

INDEX